Managing with Style

Alan J. Rowe
Richard O. Mason

Managing with Style

*A Guide to Understanding,
Assessing, and Improving
Decision Making*

 Jossey-Bass Publishers

San Francisco • London • 1987

MANAGING WITH STYLE
A Guide to Understanding, Assessing, and Improving Decision Making
by Alan J. Rowe and Richard O. Mason

Copyright © 1987 by: Jossey-Bass Inc., Publishers
                     433 California Street
                     San Francisco, California 94104
                                  &
                     Jossey-Bass Limited
                     28 Banner Street
                     London EC1Y 8QE

Excerpts from the unpublished report "CEO Management Style and the
Stages of Development in New Ventures" by J. A. Hansen are reprinted
with the permission of the author.

Excerpt from the article "Ten Rules for the CEO" by A. J. Zakon is taken
from *Annual Perspective 1983*. Copyright © 1983 by the Boston Consulting
Group. Reprinted by permission.

Library of Congress Cataloging-in-Publication Data

Rowe, Alan J.
    Managing with style.

    (Jossey-Bass management series)
    Bibliography: p.
    Includes index.
    1. Decision-making. 2. Executive ability.
I. Mason, Richard O. II. Title. III. Series.
HD30.28.R676 1987   658.4'03   87-45570
ISBN 1-55542-074-5

Manufactured in the United States of America

The paper in this book meets the guidelines for
permanence and durability of the Committee on
Production Guidelines for Book Longevity of the
Council on Library Resources.

JACKET DESIGN BY WILLI BAUM

FIRST EDITION

Code 8746

The Jossey-Bass Management Series

Consulting Editors
Organizations and Management

Warren Bennis
University of Southern California

Richard O. Mason
Southern Methodist University

Ian I. Mitroff
University of Southern California

Contents

ix

Preface

In this volume, we will explore a key factor that can contribute to career success—an individual's decision style. To be successful, an executive must know his or her style and be able to focus on achieving objectives in a frequently changing environment. In addition to knowing him- or herself, an executive must be aware of how other individuals confront and accept change and must recognize and be able to put to effective use the values and styles of these other individuals. In short, effective management requires matching the capabilities of individuals to the requirements of particular jobs. Although this may seem axiomatic, many management researchers have found that this axiom is often not followed. Many individuals hold positions or work in occupations that do not suit their personal style.

This mismatching occurs because an individual's style is not always obvious or easy to ascertain. Instead, it is often hidden, eluding all but the well-trained and observant practitioner who is able to intuit those characteristics that are most likely to lead to success. But if decision style is hidden, how does one discover one's own style, let alone that of another individual?

Over the years, a number of psychological tests have been developed to assess individual personality traits that may contribute to effective performance. We have used one such instrument, the Decision Style Inventory, to test a large number of executives in diverse organizations in order to define what attributes are needed for success. By familiarizing themselves with this inventory and the language of style, managers can learn to develop the skills necessary to perceive and understand their own and others' styles.

We all know people who perform well and gravitate toward jobs and careers compatible with their style. Two factors may influence this tendency. First, some jobs—especially high-level executive positions—have such a broad range of activities that individuals with a variety of different decision styles can be successful. Second, and far more important, some people learn to understand their style and to use it effectively. This self-knowledge gives them the power to take advantage of any given situation. It helps them persevere in those situations that require a style other than their most natural one, and it helps them create situations in which their style excels.

In addition, as *Managing with Style* will show, another benefit of mastering the language of style is that this language can shed light on many of the most perplexing problems an executive faces, including such questions as these:

1. How well does this individual's style align with the requirements of the job? And with his or her career?
   - What are the individual's strengths and weaknesses?
   - How does the individual feel about his or her co-workers?
   - How well does this individual interact and communicate with others? Can his or her communication be made more effective?
   - How results-oriented is this individual?
   - How many alternatives does the individual examine when solving problems?
   - What is this individual's risk-taking propensity?
2. Does the individual see him- or herself as others see him or her?
   - How committed is this individual to the organization?
   - How does this individual exercise power?
   - How likely is the individual to exhibit self-control?
3. How likely is this individual to be self-confident?
   - How does this individual respond to stress?
   - Does the individual prefer structure or freedom of action?
   - Does the individual seek challenges?
   - Does the individual want recognition?

4. How flexible is this individual?
   - Is this individual's thinking future-oriented?
   - Does the individual prefer tangible rewards?
   - Is this individual creative?

Although this list is not exhaustive, it helps provide an idea of the pervasiveness of decision style and its usefulness to the executive confronting his or her daily round of managerial problems.

In his extensive study of fifteen general managers, John Kotter (1982b) paints a picture of a typical workday filled with meetings, telephone conversations, and informal encounters. Managers spend most of their time with other people, both those from within and those from outside their organization, discussing an extremely wide variety of topics. Most of these conversations are short and disjointed and are initiated at someone else's request. Relatively few of these encounters are planned in advance.

The variety of the demands placed on managers does not allow them to engage in extended planning and analysis. Instead, they react to most situations based on the information at hand and their own decision style. The subconscious influence of this style infuses their response to every short meeting, every brief discussion and telephone call, and every memo dashed off to a subordinate. Even during those rare periods when a manager isolates him- or herself from others in order to engage in more thoughtful work—such as preparing budgets, formulating long-range plans, and developing organizational designs—decision style is still at work.

Overview of the Contents

In this volume we meet the needs of executives who are concerned with being more effective as well as the needs of those concerned with learning more about style and how it affects their performance and decision making. Although the examples and case studies are drawn primarily from the business world, we have found that the material covered in this book is applicable in any setting where people work together. Describing and understanding an individual human being's style is useful in predicting how that person will behave in a variety of situations, such as problem solving, motivating, leading, and so on. This insight into human behavior can benefit those who take the time and make the effort to understand and use the language of style.

Chapter One introduces the concept of decision style. Four basic decision styles are described as well as the concepts of alignment and decision situation. In Chapter Two, the biographies of several well-known executives and military leaders are used to illustrate decision style in action. Chapter Three focuses on the uses of the Decision Style Inventory and how individual scores are interpreted. And because people are far too complex to pigeonhole, style patterns—combinations of decision styles—are explained. In Chapter Four, we describe four environmental forces that affect all decision makers—work environment, peer group interaction, demands of the task to be done, and personal needs.

In Chapter Five, we use two examples to illustrate how alignment with their jobs and insight into other people's styles can affect the ways executives function. Several case studies are presented in Chapter Six to describe the key role of the executive's style and the way in which it influences the organization. Chapter Seven focuses on how to choose a meaningful career. Examples are given to show what attributes are needed to succeed in various arenas. And in Chapter Eight, four categories of executives—senior executives, staff executives, leaders, and entrepreneurs—are shown to share a common decision style.

In Chapter Nine, we examine the psychological foundations for the concept of decision style and also discuss the Myers-Briggs Type Inventory as it relates to decision style. Chapter Ten presents situation alignment, or the effect of the work environment on decision style. And finally, in Chapter Eleven, we examine the requirements of the information age and the implications that our understanding of decision styles may have for future management.

The three appendixes provide specific support for the research reported in the text: A thorough validation study is provided for those interested in the details of the testing of the Decision Style Inventory, and data are shown for two important samples of executives.

Acknowledgments

Over the past ten years, the individuals and organizations who have contributed to the research on decision styles have been far too numerous to adequately acknowledge and thank here. Those who have had a significant impact on the development of the Decision Style Inventory and the understanding of decision styles have our profound gratitude. Some of the many we want to acknowledge include Warren Bennis, James Boulgarides, Patrick Connor, Jesse Cox, Clifford Craft, Karl Dickel, Michael Driver, Gita Govani, Harold Grossman, Peter Keen, Craig Lundberg, Richard Mann, Ian Mitroff, Warren Schmidt, Hal Schutt, Ivan Somers, Judy Sparks, John Thompson, Stan Weingard, and the many executives, friends, and students who participated in the tests we conducted. Special thanks are due the Defense Systems Management College for supporting and funding research to validate and extend the findings of the Decision Style Inventory. The Army Research Institute, along with numerous organizations, patiently tested and applied the results of our decision style research. We are indebted to Tal Gilad and Cecil Johnson for painstakingly typing, retyping, and editing the drafts of the manuscript; and to Marsha Rebney and Clifford Rowe, who time and time again were willing to try each new version of the test instrument design to check for reliability and consistency. Last, but not least, we thank our wives, Helen Rowe and Foxie Mason, who put up with the endless hours we devoted to research and writing.

August 1987

Alan J. Rowe
Los Angeles, California

Richard O. Mason
Dallas, Texas

The Authors

Alan J. Rowe received his B.S. and M.S. degrees in industrial engineering from Columbia University and his Ph.D. degree in engineering and business administration from the University of California, Los Angeles. He is currently a professor of organization and management at the University of Southern California. He has published and conducted research on managerial decision making, and his work on decision styles has received worldwide recognition. Rowe has held positions on the corporate staff of General Electric, Hughes Aircraft, and Systems Development Corporation, and he has been a consultant to major U.S. companies and overseas governments. *Strategic Management and Business Policy* (1985), which Rowe coauthored with Richard O. Mason and Karl E. Dickel, has been a pacesetter in the management field.

Richard O. Mason is Carr P. Collins Distinguished Professor at the Edwin L. Cox School of Business, Southern Methodist University. He received his B.S. degree in business and technology from Oregon State University and his Ph.D. degree in business administration from the University of California, Berkeley. Mason is a council member for the Institute of Management Sciences and has served as president of the Western Academy of Management. The *Administrative Science Quarterly, Management Information Systems Quarterly, Information Society, Academy of Management Review, Human Systems Management,* and *Manage-*

ment Science are among the academic journals for which he serves as an editor or reviewer. His primary intellectual concerns revolve around strategic planning, information systems, organizations, and psychological styles. He views all of these through the philosophical lens of epistemology.

Managing with Style

1

●II●II●II●II●II●II●II●II●II●II●II●II●II●II●II●II●II●II●II●II●II●II●II●II●II●II●II●II●II●II●

Decision Style:
The Hidden Factor
in Managerial Success

A question often asked is what factors contribute to being a successful manager. The answers include talent, skill, the right experience, being energetic, being at the right place at the right time, and sometimes just plain serendipity or determination. While each of these factors can obviously contribute to success, there is a hidden factor that evades even the most perceptive person—the style that is used to accomplish important or demanding goals. What we have found is that one's style of thinking, which we call decision style, contributes to achieving those goals. This mental activity of decision style permeates everything we do. Decision style, along with the right mix of the other factors, is an essential ingredient in achieving success. Yet, because it is hidden, we may tend to ignore it, even though it is so much a part of how we think and act that it forms a fundamental base that accounts for everything that a person does.

Our interest in decision style stems from our many observations of how it affects managerial performance. We found that where style is aligned with the requirements of the job, performance is often successful, and where it is not so aligned, performance does not meet the person's potential. Our objective, then, is first to provide an understanding of what style is and then to show how it can be used. To start, we will examine a case of style in action.

1

When the Corning Glass Company was looking for an executive to lead their new thrust in the fiber optic business, they turned to Richard Dulude, an executive with a creative and entrepreneurial flair. Optical fibers clearly require an entrepreneurial spirit, explained Richard Shafer, the company's director of management and professional personnel. "We don't even know what the 'i's' and 't's' are, so we can't get someone who dots 'i's' and crosses 't's.'" Yet when the Wicks Corporation was in the throes of bankruptcy and needed a leader who could turn the company around, it sought out Sandy Sigoloff, an executive known for orderly and efficient implementation of operational objectives. Sigoloff, who is charming and friendly in person, is nevertheless a taskmaster on the job. Called "Ming the Merciless" by some former Wicks employees, he turned the company into a thriving enterprise by attention to detail and a hands-on management approach that included unannounced visits to offices and plants and tight controls on employees. Each of these executives was successful, yet each brought quite a different style to assignments. Wicks needed their "i's" dotted and "t's" crossed; Corning needed to discover theirs. Among the reasons that these executives were successful was that their style fit the needs of the organization at the time.

Decision style reflects the way that one visualizes and thinks about situations. It has to do with mental predisposition concerning personal objectives, what situations one avoids, what kinds of jobs one enjoys, what things one dislikes, how one communicates, and how one approaches problems and makes decisions. We find patterns among these predispositions that serve to describe one's style. And, since these patterns are seldom visible and rarely consciously taken into account, they are truly a hidden factor.

Nevertheless, they are ever present. When Harold Geneen, for example, declares that "Facts [are] the highest form of professional management," he is telling us a great deal about how he addresses problems and how he makes decisions. When, on the other hand, James R. Houghton, chairperson of Corning Glass Works, says, "We know in the end that the commitment and contribution of all employees will determine our success,'' he reveals something about his own decision style. It is quite obvious that Houghton's approach is quite different from Geneen's. Undoubtedly, their capability, dedication, and background contributed to their success, but hidden below the surface was the factor of style—a special way of thinking and acting that is reflected in their statements.

To understand style, one needs a language to describe and explain what it means. To meet this requirement, we have developed a set of concepts and a language that will help to explain style. The starting point was the development of an instrument called the Decision Style Inventory (DSI) used to measure one's style.

The Language of Decision Style

A language is a means used to express ideas and to communicate thoughts and feelings. So a language of style must provide concepts that can be used to describe one's mental predispositions to process information and to visualize and think about situations. To be complete, it should also be capable of describing problems confronting managers, which we call decision situations, and the environment or context in which the decision is made.

Decision Situation. There are two key dimensions that can be used to describe a decision situation—its structure and its elements. The structure may be either loose or complex. The elements are concern for people or focus on objects. Combining these two dimensions, we can define four basic categories of decision situations that confront managers. The way in which managers deal with these decision situations reflects their style.

Decision Style. There are two key aspects that describe how our mind works: its cognitive complexity and its value orientation. A person may have either a low tolerance for ambiguity (that is, a high need for structure) or a high tolerance for ambiguity. Values may be oriented either to human and social concerns or to task and technical concerns. Combining these two dimensions yields four basic styles:

1. *Directive.* This style has low tolerance for ambiguity and is oriented to task and technical concerns. A person with this style implements operational objectives in a systematic and efficient way. Sandy Sigoloff and Harold Geneen typify this style.
2. *Analytical.* This style has a high tolerance for ambiguity and is oriented to task and technical concerns. Performance is achieved by means of analysis, planning, and forecasting. The analytical and the directive styles are both logical in their approach.
3. *Conceptual.* This style has a high tolerance for ambiguity (considerable complexity) and is oriented to people and social concerns. Performance is achieved by exploring new options, forming new strategies, being creative, and taking risks. Richard Dulude typifies this style.
4. *Behavioral.* This style has a low tolerance for ambiguity and is oriented to people and social concerns. Performance is based on focusing on people and their needs. The behavioral and the conceptual styles are less logical in their approach than the directive and analytical. James Houghton typifies this style.

These four basic styles are our building blocks and are used to describe combinations of styles. A few people have only one dominant style, most people have two or three styles that dominate, and a few have balanced styles, but no one has all four as dominant.

Alignment. One achieves alignment by matching one's style with the demands of the decision structure. Alignment is achieved by either passive or active means. To achieve passive alignment, one merely finds decision situations for which one's style is well suited. This is like fitting a square peg into a matching square hole. To achieve active alignment, one reconfigures the decision environment so that one's style fits it well. Many exceptional leaders, often by dint of their willpower, have employed the active alignment approach.

Stewart Rowlings Mott is an example of an executive who has achieved alignment. He inherited a fortune from his father, who had been a major stockholder in General Motors. Having grown up with wealth and enjoying an annual income of about $1 million, his interests turned in *Buddenbrooks* fashion to human needs. His style can be described as behavioral; he has gone to great lengths to construct a working and living environment in which his style can flourish. He has become a philanthropist who uses his Park Avenue penthouse as both his office and his home. The main objects of his philanthropy are world peace and population control. But rather than deal with them on an abstract level, he focuses on individuals. "I'm no ideologue," he says. "I feel uncomfortable when asked to explain in some cogent, complete, lucid way, a blueprint of my political perceptions. I believe in chipping away at the defects in the present system without attempting to change the way it fundamentally works."

The structured and sensation-oriented aspects of Mott's style come out in his work habits. He is a voracious reader of reports, memorandums, and proposals, which flow in daily from his far-flung associations, and he sifts through all of them in order to find those individual situations that his foundation might support. As the volume of paper increases, it is sorted and stacked neatly around the perimeter of the room that he makes his main office. "I don't know how to throw things out," he reflects, "people, old newspapers or cigarette boxes." And yet he is a friendly and happy person who is highly enthusiastic about what he does. With the aid of his wealth and with an exceptional intuitive understanding of the needs of his style, Stewart Mott has created an environment in which he excels.

Decision Style Inventory (DSI). The Decision Style Inventory is an instrument that is used to classify people according to the four basic styles. It also reveals complex patterns of styles, showing dominant and backup styles. As is evident, decision style is just one of a number of ways an executive can identify what is required to achieve success. Yet we believe that the concept of decision style and the Decision Style Inventory can make valuable contributions to the executive's managerial understanding. The concept of decision style helps executives understand people's mental predispositions, why they perceive things a

certain way, and why they act accordingly. It also helps executives to understand differences in the way people approach
their jobs. The Decision Style Inventory taps into the hidden
recesses of a person's mind and helps to explain a person's style.
The concept of decision style and the use of the Decision Style
Inventory provide a language for examining style and for ap-
preciating the vital role it plays in our daily lives.

The language of decision style is useful at several levels.
For each individual, it can be used to understand oneself and
to determine whether one is well suited for a current position
or career. For a group, the language helps to clarify similarities
and differences in style among its members; this information
can be used to improve communications and coordination within
an organization. Finally, the language of decision style can be
used by senior executives to determine the match between the
style of individuals in the organization and the tasks to which
they are assigned.

How Style Is Used

High-performing organizations are generally led by executives who can visualize requirements, take risks, and make
difficult choices to deal with the many complex situations that
confront them. For example, J. Peter Grace, one of the country's longest-reigning chief executives, has been known to stop
at a coffee shop, like it, visualize its potential, and, after some
research, take action by buying the entire chain. This is a classic
example of a person with both a conceptual style—seeing the
whole picture—and a directive style—taking action that leads
to implementation. While most corporate executives need to involve their boards of directors and even consider their stockholders before making decisions such as Grace's, here is an example of a forceful leader who "makes decisions."

Another example of this decision style is Roy Ash.
Addressograph-Multigraph International moved to Los Angeles
from Cleveland after Ash became its chairperson. He explained,
"putting the company close to high technology centers would
help it expand in that direction." Of course, the rationale for
the decision was sound, but is that all there was to it? Or was

it perhaps significant that Ash knew the Los Angeles area, had been a senior executive at Litton Industries for many years, and had enjoyed living in the Los Angeles area? Ironically, shortly after he was replaced by Richard Black as chairperson of Ad- dressograph-Multigraph, the company moved to Chicago— Richard Black's hometown.

How often is rationalization stemming from one's style and personal needs used to justify a major decision by senior executives? Can we use decision styles to help predict such actions? While Grace appears to have a directive style, both Ash and Black also had this style. They all demonstrated "forceful" directive action, a style that made their conceptual "vision" a reality. Do all senior executives make decisions this way? It would be foolish to suggest that there is a stereotypical senior executive, because so much depends on the environment and circumstances in which style is used. Lee Iacocca was able to take a moribund Chrysler Corporation and revitalize it to become an effective competitor with Ford and General Motors. The situation at Chrysler demanded a forceful visionary. Iacocca rose to the challenge and accepted only one dollar as pay his first year—he was willing to take risks. Undaunted by the magnitude of the task, Iacocca added the responsibility of chairing the Statue of Liberty fund-raising drive and again was a howling, though controversial, success.

Were these exceptional executives born that way, or is it that they fit the times? Was it alignment—the matching of decision style to the environmental demands—that made them successful? There is case after case of executives who understood themselves, had high positive self-regard, and understood the environment in which they worked who have pursued brilliant careers. Can anyone do this? We believe that it is possible for each of us to develop our potential to manage more effectively. If you understand yourself, understand others, recognize environmental demands, and are able to obtain commitment from the individuals in the organization who can help meet those demands, you are a strong candidate for being a successful executive. Where does decision style fit? It provides the insights that help us understand ourselves and others (Hall, 1984).

Managing an organization successfully requires more than personality or energy or intelligence. Managers must be able to interact with individuals both inside and outside of the organization. They must make decisions that go against the grain of staff advice, and they must have the vision to see opportunity and potential where none existed before. How can we use what we know about style to determine how executives manage their organizations?

Understanding Our Own Style

How can a knowledge of decision style be valuable to you? Why should one learn about his or her own style or the style of others? There are at least four good reasons: When we understand our own and others' styles, (1) we understand ourselves better, (2) we understand others better, (3) we better understand organizations and their managerial needs, and (4) we are in a better position to design organizations that can effectively cope with external conditions.

Most of our lives, we do the things that come naturally without reflecting on them very much. Sometimes these habits work for us, and sometimes they do not. We seldom know why. The language of style helps us to understand the reasons for these successes and failures and provides some clues as to how and what to change. Knowing our style, we are in a position to determine our strengths and to identify those parts of our potential that are underdeveloped—what Jung called our "inferior functions." Armed with this potential for self-improvement, with a perspective that emphasizes strengths and reduces weaknesses, we are able to avoid situations for which our style is not well suited.

Donna Dower, a doctoral candidate, was studying and teaching accounting. Her style was not very analytical—considerably less analytical than that of a "typical" accountant. In conversations with her, we suggested that her highly conceptual style would indicate a preference for another occupation. Very upset, she responded, "I love accounting and I intend pursuing it as my career." When asked what she liked about accounting, she replied, "I guess it's not accounting that I like, but rather bookkeeping." We then asked her how bookkeeping differed from accounting. Dower replied, "The reason I prefer bookkeeping is that it gives me the flexibility of deciding how to set up the books, whereas accounting is too rigid and has too many rules." Once we went beyond the semantic difficulty, the problem was resolved. Dower preferred the freedom of action that is typical of a highly conceptual style. Here is a classic case of a person with a conceptual style in a profession that typically requires a strong analytical style. On the other hand, because of her broad perspective, Dower is the kind of individual who can make a valuable contribution to the field of accounting by going beyond the rules. Another accountant, the daughter of a navy admiral, also had a high conceptual style. When we suggested that she might want to become an artist, she laughed and said that she was an artist, even though her mother objected; accounting was only a job that she did to earn money. She understood her style and recognized that artists usually are a starving lot, which did not appeal to her. A similar example is an airline pilot at Tiger International, who also had a high conceptual style, who said that flying gave him the income and flexibility to pursue his other interests. He also saw his job as a means to the end of personal freedom that so many conceptual people desire.

Alignment of Style

When people's style is aligned to the tasks that they are undertaking, a transcendental flow is established between them and their work. In this state of alignment, they become "at one" with their work. People who reach this state describe it as euphoric. Athletes reach a state of alignment occasionally; superior athletes reach it often. Larry Bird, the great Boston Celtics forward, is one of those exceptional athletes whose whole being is wrapped up in the game of basketball. On the court, he becomes totally absorbed in the game to the point where he no longer thinks about it but acts instinctively. A quick pass without looking to Kevin McHale just as he pivots away for a defender caught in a pick set by Robert Parrish, an unexpected move into the passing lane to intercept an opponent's pass, a counter-flow movement that leaves him standing alone to grab a rebound from an opponent's errant shot—these are some of the sub-conscious moves that Bird makes easily because he is so involv-ed with the game.

Tennis player Tim Gallwey reports the very same ex-perience. He refers to the altered state of consciousness that one achieves in a perfect state of alignment as the "inner game of tennis." In the inner game, time is redefined, and one's senses are highly sharpened. The opponent's power serve is observed as if it were a series of still photographs clipped from a motion picture. The fuzz and the seams of the ball are in perfect relief as its spin reveals itself directly to the player's muscles as they gradually position the racket for the return volley. The mind is at rest, and it somehow encompasses the server, the ball, the net, and everything of relevance on the court while at the same time excluding anything that is not essential to the moment. This is the state in which one's performance reaches its highest peak.

Understanding Others

There are many different contexts in which people find themselves. Some, for example, require an ability to understand and empathize with others, as James Houghton's philosophy suggests. Some demand technical and analytical capabilities, as in Harold Geneen's organization. Moreover, some situations are vague and ill defined, while others are well structured. To be effective, one must understand the nature of the environ-ment in which one operates. "Fit," then, is the match between one's style and the demands of the situation.

"Fully 80 percent of all American workers in every job category may have jobs for which they are unsuited," observes consulting psychologist Harry Levinson in explaining the need to fit an executive's style to the demands of an organization at a given time (Levinson, 1981, p. 296). Sigoloff's emphasis on pushing production and cutting costs probably might not have worked at Corning when the company attempted to get its fledgling fiber optics business started. But then Dulude's entrepreneurial flair for development of a new technology was not the need at Wicks either. As it turned out, each executive was well suited for the job he undertook. This condition, in which one's style is effectively matched with the demands of the environment in which one must act, is alignment. When people find themselves in situations where their style is inappropriately aligned with the demands of the environment, they will begin to perform poorly and become dissatisfied. This leads to negative reinforcement, which results in a loss of self-confidence, reduced commitment, and lower motivation, in turn leading to even lower performance and lower satisfaction. On the other hand, if there is a good fit between one's style and the situation, this leads to a positive feedback cycle, with increased self-confidence, higher motivation, and deeper commitment, which result in better performance and satisfaction. In the search for these positive outcomes, the hidden factor of style can be helpful. When faced with decision situations for which their style is mismatched, people who are otherwise competent will often fail. Our studies have shown that sustaining high performance demands a style in alignment with the task to be performed. This, then, has significant implications for the selection of jobs and careers.

The Case of Spectronics

As president and founder of Spectronics, located in the Dallas, Texas, area, Tom Gardner found that drive and dedication were not enough to achieve goals. Spectronics manufactured spectrometer and electron microscope interfaces that Gardner had developed. The company began, as many entrepreneurial organizations do, in an old auto repair shop. By 1984, Spectronics had reached close to $200 million in sales, with offices in Europe, Japan, and Hong Kong. Peter Oster was one of Gardner's first employees, hired as manager of international marketing. From all outward appearances, Oster was quite successful in the job. He was adept at working with bureaucrats in Paris, Dusseldorf, and London. He was very comfortable meeting with political dignitaries throughout Europe. He was also exceptionally knowledgeable about Spectronics's products and their applications. During Oster's tenure, several government agencies had purchased a considerable amount of Spectronics's equipment.

When the corporate vice-president of marketing retired, Gardner almost immediately appointed Oster to replace him. Oster, in his eyes, was loyal, knowledgeable, and capable of running a successful operation. Soon after the appointment, Oster moved his family back to the United States and assumed his new responsibilities. Within his first few months on the job, however, Gardner discovered that Oster was having difficulty preparing budgets and forecasts for several new products. Gardner's response was to bring in a marketing consultant to help Oster prepare the necessary documents. The consultant devised an improved product sales forecasting system, but even with the new system, the sales budgets and forecast documents were running considerably behind schedule. A month later, virtually no progress had been made. Concerned, Gardner visited Oster's office to discuss the problem with him. Near the end of their meeting, he set a deadline for completing the documents. Oster said that he simply could not complete the documents within that short a time period because of his heavy work load. Gardner volunteered to assist, but Oster still maintained that he needed more time. Frustrated, Gardner left Oster's office.

Upon returning to his own office, Gardner made a few phone calls and soon discovered that several of the company's key salespeople were displeased with Oster's leadership. They complained that he was not providing them with very much guidance for selling and marketing the new product line. He would not make sales calls with them and was not making the decisions they needed to move aggressively on some major accounts. This information deepened Gardner's concern. Suspecting that personal problems might be the cause of Oster's inaction, he discreetly investigated Oster's personal life. He could find no evidence of gambling, drinking, or drugs. Moreover, Oster's marriage appeared to be strong and loving. The couple were seen together frequently, and they were active participants in their son's soccer league, attending most of the games.

Gardner was perplexed as he reflected on Oster's career. He had known and worked with Oster since founding the company. From the beginning, Oster had always been a loyal, hard worker and a seemingly competent manager. As the company grew and as Oster assumed more responsibility, he seemed to handle matters effectively. While on the European assignment, which had been a big jump at the time, he had seemed to perform well. Now it was clear that he was performing poorly as vice-president of marketing. Moreover, the harder Gardner pushed Oster, the more difficult the situation became. Gardner wondered why.

Oster was assigned to a job that did not fit his conceptual decision style. The demands of the job forced him to do things that he was uncomfortable doing, and, as a consequence, the events in his new assignment put impossible pressure on him. In response, he retreated more deeply into his natural conceptual style and became generally less effective. Gardner's high expectations drove Oster even further into his basic style and served to exacerbate his difficulties.

As part of a training program, Oster had taken the Decision Style Inventory. His decision style was typical of persons who favored gregariousness, politeness, and cautiousness—a style that we call behavioral. His other style—one that we call conceptual—is the product of an inquiring and curious mind, for Oster enjoyed new ideas and fresh approaches to problems. People with this combination of styles generally abhor working with numbers and formulas. They seldom take action quickly, and they avoid confronting aggressive people with opposing points of view. Oster's decision style had been appropriate for his assignment in Europe, where his social skills and easygoing ways exactly matched the continent's business conventions. The vice-president's job, however, forced him to draw on other dimensions of his mental capacities, with which he was much less comfortable. Analyzing sales reports and dealing with demanding salespeople were not natural or enjoyable tasks for Oster. So he avoided doing these things and concentrated on things that came easier to him, such as thinking about new marketing ideas and establishing relationships with trade associations.

As a consequence of this lack of alignment between style and job demands, his performance deteriorated, at least in Gardner's eyes and those of Spectronics sales personnel. Aware of this problem, Oster sought to do the things he did best—talking to people with whom he was at ease and thinking about broader aspects of the business. Under pressure, Oster thus initiated a destructive psychological feedback cycle. In the face of great stress, he continued to do fewer of the things that the vice-president's job called for (and that Gardner expected of him) and more of the things that were consistent with his basic decision style. This cycle was broken only after each of the two executives became aware of the psychological binds that they had created for themselves. When Gardner was shown results of Oster's Decision Style Inventory and understood some of its implications, he realized that the very tendencies that he had seen as strengths in Oster were in reality limitations in his new assignment. Gardner recalled, for example, that during his European assignment, Oster had conceived of the marketing approach and had made initial contacts with high-level government officials. When it came down to "real selling," however, all of the tough negotiations and the final closing of the deals had been accomplished by another sales representative. "In fact," Gardner recollected, "I don't know that Peter has actually ever closed a deal which required direct selling. He is a good idea man, a valuable resource because of his knowledge of the business, and an excellent contact generator. But he is not a hard-nosed salesman and, come to think of it, he is no detail man either—hates numbers, budgets, and reports." It was clear to Gardner that Oster's style was not the right match for the job of vice-president of marketing as he had defined it.

In a conversation that we had with Gardner, he agreed that the decision to put Oster in the vice-president's job had resulted in a considerable loss in sales, a high price for a young company with growth aspirations. Gardner wondered why he had made the decision. When he was shown the results of his own Decision Style Inventory, however, the answer emerged. Gardner exhibited an analytical and conceptual style, with much stronger directive tendencies than Oster had. This is a style pattern that we often find associated with senior executives. It is a style that emphasizes developing plans, finding solutions, making quick decisions, and expecting practical results. These characteristics were so much a part of Gardner that they were implicit in everything he did. He unconsciously looked for people who could meet these requirements in the job. In effect, Gardner was looking for a person with his own characteristics to fill the vice-president's job. But Oster was not another Gardner. He had a different decision style. Oster had valuable skills, which Gardner admired, and he was devoted and loyal to the company, which Gardner demanded, but his style was not compatible with Gardner's expectations. As this difference in styles became apparent to Gardner, he began to rethink the role of vice-president of marketing in the company. In order to take advantage of Oster's strengths, the vice-president's job was redefined to include more public relations, coordinations, and long-range technological assessments. A general sales manager job was created to which many of the budgeting and direct sales management responsibilities were assigned.

When we discussed Oster's style with him, he saw how it related to Gardner's. This discussion helped Oster see the trap he had created for himself by retreating into the style that he was most comfortable with rather than dealing directly with the mismatch (lack of alignment) between his preferred style and the demands of the job. He was thus better able to understand the more action-oriented and analytical demands of a senior executive's job.

Spectronics's senior management team is functioning much more smoothly today because of the organizational changes made in the vice-president of marketing's job and the deeper understanding that both Gardner and Oster have regarding their differences in style. Most importantly, Oster has become effective again and now enjoys his job. Throughout Spectronics, decision style is used as a "language" that helps executives to understand and manage people better.

Decision Style in an Information Society

The language of decision style is becoming essential to management in the emerging information age. In 1980, the

United States became the first nation in which the majority of those employed were "knowledge workers." Other Western countries are rapidly following suit. Knowledge workers include professional, managerial, technical, and clerical workers—people whose main contribution consists of collecting, processing, and communicating information. Knowledge work is an intensely mental process. The mind of one person affects the minds of others by the communications that take place. As a consequence of its psychological nature, knowledge work presents many new challenges to management. This type of job will increasingly rely on decision style as a key determinant of success, as is evident from a brief review of the events leading up to the information age.

As late as the early 1900s, the majority of Americans made their living on the farm. Agriculture consisted primarily of hard work and farming skill. As a consequence, a farmer's psychological predisposition was not critical to success. With the turn of the century came the beginning of industrialization and the building of large manufacturing plants. People migrated from farms to the cities, where psychological factors were to play a more important role than they did on the farm. Elton Mayo, Fritz Roethlisberg, and Will Dickson (Roethlisberg and Dickson, 1939) discovered this at the Western Electric Hawthorne plant near Chicago. In industrial plants, much of the work places physical demands on the individual. For example, an activity such as assembling motors requires specific skills and physical effort. In these industrial settings, attitudes, motivation, and social control played an important role in performance—managers clearly needed to know about them—but, because of the nature of factory work, a deep understanding of mental predisposition of workers was seldom used by managers. For over fifty years, industrial workers, mostly semiskilled machine operators, were the largest single class of workers in the United States.

A significant change occured in 1960, when the U.S. Census Bureau reported that those employees designated as knowledge workers had become the single largest class in the United States. Today, knowledge workers constitute the majority of employed people in America. Managers and professionals, in particular, have comparatively greater discretion in what they do than did the farm workers. Most of their work goes on in their minds, hidden from observation by others. Decision style, thus, is more relevant in this kind of work. As a consequence, decision style has now become one of the key factors contributing to success.

Knowledge workers inhabit a strange new world, one that is socially defined and psychologically administered. The way they think about problems, the way they communicate with others, and their expectations of others materially affect their performance. These are the very factors that the concept of decision style captures. In fact, decision style relates to almost every aspect of a knowledge worker's job. It influences how information is organized in one's mind—serially, spatially, or behaviorally—and how one reacts to stimuli—with precepts, insight, instinct, or intuition. Moreover, responses to stress are generally different for each decision style. Recall that Oster reacted to the stress of his new assignment by avoidance and retreat, whereas Gardner became annoyed and began to establish deadlines. In general, knowledge workers' jobs are characterized by heavy mental activity, socially induced stress, and conflicting motivations. Because of the flexibility that they have in doing their work, there are manifold opportunities for mismatches in jobs and misunderstandings among people, the very problems that Gardner and Oster experienced at Spectronics.

To make these ideas come to life, we will describe in the next chapter several executives and leaders with different styles, all of whom succeeded in what they did by effective use of style. When we describe these exceptional people, it will become obvious why the language of decision style is valuable to explain how people function in organizations.

2

●II●II●II●II●II●II●II●II●II●II●II●II●II●II●II●II●II●II●II●II●II●II●II●II●II●II●II●II●II●

Four Elements of Style:
Analytical, Conceptual
Behavioral, Directive

Decision style is the way that we perceive and comprehend stimuli and how we choose to respond. Robert McNamara used it to analyze and systematize the U.S. defense establishment during the early 1960s. Edwin Land used it when he invented the Polaroid camera and created an organization to manufacture and sell it. Alfred Marrow used it when he took a strife-torn Harwood Manufacturing Company, democratized it, humanized it, and turned it into a profitable company. And Harold Geneen used it when he took firm control of ITT Corporation and directed it into one of the largest corporations in the world.

Each managed with a different style. Each was exceedingly successful in achieving his goals. Each managed one or more major institutions, and each had an impact on the world of management. And yet each in his own way exhibited great limitations. This is the essential characteristic of style. It is the predisposition of a person to think and to act in a specific way in a given situation—a preferred mode of thinking, often to the exclusion of others. The manner of thinking or focusing determines one's inherent ability to manage effectively. These attributes often are considered part of the human experience.

"Why is it," the ancient Greek philosopher Theophrastus mused in his book on *Characters,* "that while all Greece lies under the same sky, and all the Greeks are educated alike, it has befallen us to have characters variously constituted?'' Why is it, we might ask, that executives such as McNamara, Land, Marrow, and Geneen exhibit such differences in the way they manage? There is something programmed within us, deep within the recesses of our minds, that causes us to view the world in different ways and to react accordingly. Its source is unknown, and its essential character is undefinable. Yet we know that it exists and, what is more important, that there are certain discernible patterns of style that occur over and over again in the general population. It is the consistency of pattern that helps us to understand style and to determine whether one's style fits a given situation. As noted in the previous chapter, matching an individual's style to the task or job, including the work environment, is crucial to effective performance. When there is a misfit, everything seems to go wrong. A match leads us to be energized and derive meaning, substance, and satisfaction from what we do. These beneficial experiences become powerful contributers to our performance in an organization and reinforce the satisfaction that we derive from the work performed. In turn, the organization is given life and form and the psychic power necessary to work effectively. In essence, style is the soul of leadership. This proposition can best be illustrated by contrasting different styles.

Patton and Bradley: Contrasts in Style

Screaming sirens filled the cool Georgia air, announcing the arrival of General George S. Patton, Jr. It was January 15, 1942, and Patton was about to assume command of the First Armored Corps at Fort Benning. A vanguard of motorcyclists with sirens blasting, helmets gleaming, rifles polished, and flags ready for raising secured the headquarters area. These were followed by two tanks and two troop carriers complete with fully uniformed, battle-ready soldiers. Patton arrived standing erect in his command car just a few minutes before the new orders were official. At the precise moment that they did become official, he ordered ''Sergeant! Post the Colors!'' and then he spoke: ''We are in for a long war against a tough enemy. We must train millions of men to be soldiers. We must make them tough in mind and body, and they must be trained to kill. As officers we must give leadership in becoming tough physically and mentally. Every man in this command must be able to run a mile in fifteen minutes with full military pack!'' To a few disgruntled soldiers, he retorted, ''Damn it! I mean every man! Every officer and enlisted man, staff and command, every man will run a mile! We will start running from this point in exactly thirty minutes! I will lead!'' (Williamson, 1979, p. 26)

''A commander will command!'' This was one of Patton's inviolable principles and a central tenet of his decision style. It was a necessary style, military historians argue, for directing the great sweep of the Third Army across France in the summer of 1944 and for overcoming the staunch resistance led by German Field Marshal Gerd von Runstedt. That campaign was crucial for the Allies' victory in Europe. Considered to be aggressive and domineering by his men—they either loved or hated him—''Old Blood and Guts'' directed his tank attacks with initiative, ruthlessness, and virtual disregard for traditional military rules. Though not the ideal image for a professional military officer, this was the type of leadership needed to confront and push back an entrenched German army. In short, Patton was the right man for the job. Despite their reservations, Generals Eisenhower and Bradley intuitively understood this and supported his command.

General Omar Bradley, on the other hand, displayed a very different style. Cautious and deliberate, though imaginative and open-minded, Bradley approached the responsibility of command from a different point of view. Discussing MacArthur's command in Korea, Bradley said, ''You can't run a campaign unless you have the feel of it, and you can't get the feel of it seven miles away.'' The doctrine is absolutely sound. ''You don't even tell a corps or division commander how to do his job when you have an army. You assign a mission, and it's up to the fellow to carry it out. Of course, if you are in a position to have a look and talk it over with the guy, you make suggestions, but he doesn't have to take them.'' Bradley was so faithful to this principle that, according to a colonel on Patton's staff, when he was reduced to a "one-army Army Group" during the Ardennes battle, he declined to interfere with the tactics of that army, the Third. According to the colonel, Bradley told Patton, "It's your army, George. You fight it" (Liebling, 1951, p. 48).

It was this broad perspective on command and this breadth of vision that made Bradley the appropriate commander to lead the united First, Third, Ninth, and Fifteenth armies during the crucial latter episodes of the European campaign. Bradley had a deeper understanding of people and a broader conception of war and of peace than did Patton. This difference in style made him a valuable leader in many ways. As World War II drew to a close, Bradley was called upon to assume several important statesmanlike positions, including becoming the first chair of the newly formed Joint Chiefs of Staff and overseeing the unification of the armed services in 1949. Omar Bradley, too, was the right person at the right time for the job.

Patton and Bradley. Two totally different military styles, yet each appropriate and effective in its own way. McNamara, Land, Marrow, and Geneen. Four quite different styles of management, but each a good match for the time, place, and context in which it was employed. What can we learn from these lessons of stylisitc fit? For over a decade, we have pursued this question. We have examined the styles of leaders at many levels in management, government, and other organizations. We have discussed and debated the topic with students, colleagues, and executives. And we have developed a decision style instrument—to be described in the next chapter—and administered it to a very large number of people in various walks of life. From these endeavors, we have distilled a mass of observations down to four essential and fundamental styles that serve as primary building blocks for the concept of style. These four styles—analytical, behavioral, conceptual, and directive—are the cornerstones of the language of style. They are used to identify patterns and combinations of styles and to highlight similarities and differences among styles. In the following sections of this chapter, we examine the basic styles by means of examples.

Robert McNamara: The Analytical Style

Robert McNamara's dominant basic style can be described as analytical. "Computer Bob," as the press called him, was one of the "Whiz Kids" who with Tex Thornton and Roy Ash executed a total turnaround of the Ford Motor Company during the 1950s. Soon after John F. Kennedy was elected U.S. President in 1960, he turned to McNamara to help rationalize the shapeless and bloating military-industrial complex that had grown up in the aftermath of the Second World War. McNamara became Kennedy's secretary of defense and later also served President Lyndon Johnson. He ruled the Department of Defense longer and reportedly more efficiently than any other secretary.

During his tenure, McNamara became well known for his careful analysis, his thirst for accurate and complete data to feed his analyses, his ability to evaluate multiple options, and his unrelenting quest for the best possible solution to any problem he undertook. Upon his resignation as secretary of defense in December 1967, *Life* magazine summarized his management style: "McNamara's mind is able to devour mountains of facts, apply reason and produce decisions on everything from which war plane or missile to build, to ways of streamlining the procurement of belt buckles. He expounds these decisions in his schoolmasterly way—with equal sureness to military brass, foreign VIPs, congressmen and Presidents. His decisions have sometimes been wrong and—right or wrong—not always appreciated" ("Big Shoes for the U.S. to Fill," 1967, p. 35)

This behavior is exemplary of the analytical style, which is characterized by a capacity for abstract and logical thinking and a high tolerance for ambiguity. The analytical style seeks to bring order to chaos by modeling and shaping information so that the mind is able to grasp its many dimensions. This McNamara did at the Department of Defense. Lyndon Johnson once remarked that McNamara was the only person who ever understood the "Puzzle of the Pentagon." The analytical style's creation of a mental model of a situation requires verifying and understanding considerable amounts of data. This McNamara did with alacrity. When confronting him at a budget hearing, General Curtis

LeMay acknowledged that he was astounded at McNamara's detailed knowledge of the defense budget.

The analytical thinker generally tries to gain the broadest possible perspective of a problem, seeks to identify previously "taken for granted" underlying assumptions, exposes these assumptions to examination, and then argues for a new set of assumptions. This style tends to use a rather formal decision-making process, in which many possible alternatives are envisioned, each is carefully examined, and an evaluation is conducted to determine the optimal policy to follow. McNamara followed this formal model perhaps as closely as it is possible to do in many pressing management situations. He also displayed another characteristic of the analytical style: he enjoyed variety. Interspersed with all this intensive problem solving were quiet moments with his family in Ann Arbor, Michigan, reading Robert Frost's poetry aloud; frequent debates with the intellectuals in his hometown about issues that he was addressing in Washington; and an occasional hike in the California Sierras. Hiking was a challenge for him, just like trying to wrestle with the complexities of defense. And this, too, is characteristic of the analytical style.

Edwin Land: The Conceptual Style

Edwin Land, as was General Omar Bradley, is an archetype of the conceptual style. As a scientist and inventor, he has been compared favorably to Thomas Edison, Alexander Graham Bell, and the pioneer of photography, George Eastman. Each had the creative capacity to envision a new technology and the managerial comprehension to create the organizational structures necessary to bring it to the marketplace. Land was largely self-taught. His first breakthrough as a scientist came when, as a young man of seventeen, he left a dark New York restaurant and started down Broadway. As he turned down the street, he was met by that continual flow of bright headlights that so characterize nighttime traffic in New York City. The glare almost blinded him. Stunned and mesmerized, he closed his eyes and began to turn over solutions to the problem in his head. Human

beings shouldn't have to put up with this, he thought. In a flash
of insight, an answer occured to him. Perhaps polarizing filters
would eliminate the headlight glare.

The year was 1926, and Edwin Land was just a freshman
at Harvard. But with this intuition firmly in his mind, he laid
out a rather complete life plan. He quit Harvard—the rules and
constraints bothered him anyway—and set up his own little
laboratory. His first solution was to produce polarized headlights
and windshields, but patent problems emerged, and because
of his youth, he ran into great difficulty obtaining the financial
support he needed. Undaunted, he sought another application
for his idea. Sunglasses were his next attempt, and this time
he succeeded. By the outbreak of World War II, Land had
established a small firm that made and sold polarized sunglasses
and was enjoying a steadily increasing market. During the war,
his firm turned its efforts to developing optical devices for military applications. This could have been the end of the story,
were it not for a rather remarkable event.

After the war, Land took his daughter Jenny on a trip
to New Mexico, where they hiked, fished, and rode horse-
back. Always present on these treks was a camera, for he wanted
to preserve the fun and warm feelings of those moments together so that he might live them again when they returned
to New York. Jenny, however, had a different idea. She wanted
to see the pictures "right now" and grew impatient as he tried
to explain about film developing and the time it took to process photos. Something about her pleas struck deep within
him. Many other people, he speculated, must share Jenny's
feelings. They too must be impatient at the long delay between
the click of the shutter and the viewing of the result. As the
two hiked back to their hotel in Santa Fe, ideas began to play
in his mind. He apparently worked out the entire design for
the Polaroid instant camera in a little over an hour. By 1948,
he had conceived, created, produced, and marketed the first
instant camera in the world. "I was able to construct the whole
scheme and define all the variables [in my mind]," he wrote,
upon retiring as chief executive officer of Polaroid Corporation in 1980. "It was a delightful, scientific problem" (Bello,
1959, p. 158).

Land loved to work with people who were curious and open-minded, people, as he described it, who had a "sparkle in their eye." Like Omar Bradley, he gave the people who worked for him considerable autonomy—his associates cannot recall his every having given a single order. This humanistic aspect of his decision style paid off well on several occasions. In fact, it was responsible for the development of many of Polaroid's film products. For example in 1948 Land hired Meroe Morse, the daughter of a Princeton mathematician, who had just received an arts degree from Smith College. Morse became one of Land's closest associates. She was placed in charge of all film research at Polaroid, and Land never interfered with her responsibilities. During her tenure, the research laboratory produced many new ideas and products.

A perfectionist, Land felt that it was necessary "to work intensely for long hours when beginning to see solutions to a problem. At such times atavistic competences seem to well up. You are handling so many variables at a barely conscious level that you can't afford to be interrupted. If you are, it may take a year to cover the same ground you could otherwise in sixty hours" (Bello, 1959, p. 158).

A deep intuitive contact with the minds of past generations—Carl Jung called it the "collective unconscious"—is a central characteristic of the conceptual style. It is revealed in individuals who have high cognitive complexity and a high tolerance for ambiguity. People who have a conceptual style are broad "systems" thinkers who have expansive time horizons. They are able to deal with the past, the present, and the future simultaneously. Psychologically, as Elliot Jaques aptly phrased it, they have the longest "time span of discretion" (Jaques, 1982, p. 130). They also generally have the greatest geographical reach and comprehension.

People who have a conceptual style tend to value quality and, like Land, Bradley, and, to some extent, Peter Oster at Spectronics, prefer openness, curiosity, and a sharing of values among their colleagues. Characterized by a high need for achievement, this style requires recognition, praise, and constructive feedback. Most of all, however, the conceptual style needs freedom. Edwin Land cherished his freedom to explore, to think,

and to express himself as he saw fit more dearly than any other
value. It was an important part of his career, and he steadfastly
refused to relinquish it no matter how much pressure he was
under. A person with a dominant conceptual style, we have
found, must have independence and a relatively unfettered opportunity to pursue personal goals if his or her full creative potential is to be realized.

Alfred Marrow: The Behavioral Style

Alfred J. Marrow is perhaps the least well known of our
four archetypes. His style was predominantly behavioral, and,
as we will discuss in subsequent chapters, the behavioral style
is the least prevalent among the executive styles, especially
among leaders in Western countries. Marrow was president and
chairperson of the board of the Harwood Manufacturing Company of Marion, Virginia, from 1940 until 1976. Harwood is
a successful manufacturer of men's pajamas and shorts and
children's middy blouses. Its gross sales are over $3 million a
year. The Marion plant has been in operation since 1939 and
grew to about 650 employees during Marrow's tenure. It became
the proving ground for his theories of management.

Marrow's approach to management was primarily based
on his behavioral style, which is intensely personal, focusing
on the individual as the fundamental entity in an organization,
and is characterized as supportive, empathetic, informal, and
participative. He took great pride in developing a person's
capabilities and career path. He contended that what was best
for the individual was also best for Harwood. This belief led
him to pioneer many humanistic management approaches. One
technique that he used successfully was to bring together all of
the employees who worked on a product line several times a
week to discuss problems, opportunities, and or personal issues
concerning its manufacture. This technique foreshadowed the
Japanese concept of "quality circles" and was based on Marrow's belief that the worker "on the spot" was in the best position to know about problems and solutions and that every employee should have an area of decision making that could be
considered his or her own.

An effective employee, in his view, would be able to identify with the final output of his or her work and to relate what
is done on the job to his or her social life. All critical issues at
Harwood, such as wage disputes and the failure to meet production schedules, were solved by "group discussions." A "full
disclosure" policy was also initiated. When new employees came
on board, an empathetic interviewer would tell them what the
job was "really like." The work was mostly monotonous, noisy,
and tiring, and it would be that way until the new employee
would get used to it. They were also told how some of the other
workers coped with these conditions and whom to go to for help.
The purpose of this policy was to demonstrate the company's
personal concern for employees' well-being and to provide personal support and "ego involvement" in the job.

Confronted with problems of high turnover at the plant
in 1944, Marrow responded with one of the most innovative
approaches in the history of management. He sensed that the
underlying cause was psychological rather than economic or
operational. This led him to seek the advice of one of the leading
psychologists of the day, Kurt Lewin of the Massachusetts Institute of Technology. The two commenced a thorough study
of all aspects of the plant, focusing primarily on the people and
their feelings. As Marrow reported in a paper that he delivered
at the National Vocational Guidance Association Convention
in Chicago in March of 1948 (Marrow, 1948), they began their
inquiry by theorizing that the high turnover was a symptom
of a "feeling of failure" on the part of the workers rather than
being due primarily to the more culturally acceptable reasons,
such as wage rates, that leaving employees gave in their ter-
minal interviews. They felt this to be true despite the fact that
not a single employee in the company's history had stated that
the reason for quitting was a feeling of failure to meet production quotas. Pursuing this hypothesis, Lewin and Marrow were
able to collect data that proved their point.

During the preceding month, none of the 116 employees
who produced above standard, which was sixty units an hour,
had quit. However, 28 (13 percent) of the 211 of those who produced below standard had quit. In-depth interviews revealed
that frustration was the most frequent reason for quitting. They

reasoned that a worker's frustration and fear of failure would be reduced if the worker participated in the setting of his or her own production quota and that this process could be more personal, compassionate, and supportive than the impersonal handing down of standards by cost accountants. The method they devised was to have trainers meet individually with each worker and jointly agree to a mutually satisfactory production goal. By the use of this method—which anticipated management by objectives—turnover at Harwood declined by over 50 percent while productivity increased significantly.

Marrow summarized some of his experiences at Harwood in his book *Behind the Executive Mask* (Marrow, 1964), which became the first handbook on sensitivity training. Management would be significantly improved, in his opinion, if management and the workers came together in a benign and protected setting in which they could openly share their experiences. It was hoped that during these sessions people would reveal their inner feelings so that these could be discussed, examined, and if necessary "repaired." In this way, the participants could go away refreshed and cleansed of counterproductive attitudes and feelings.

In addition to his reputation as a humanist and as a manager, Marrow was also an avid listener who was exceptionally effective in group meetings. This is undoubtedly one of the reasons New York mayor Wagner appointed him to chair the New York Commission on Intergroup Relations in 1955. In announcing the appointment, Wagner explicitly recognized Marrow's special talent for making practical application of his scholarly expertise in group dynamics and in industrial relations. Marrow was known for applying his knowledge of how to achieve participatory democracy in the groups with whom he worked to all his endeavors. Not only was this philosophy deeply felt and followed in his own affairs, but it was also the standard by which he judged others. In 1974, about four years before his death, Alfred Marrow rocked the audience at the symposium held on the occasion of the fiftieth anniversary of the original Hawthorne studies at Oakbrook, Illinois, with a scathing denouncement of the humanistic and political practices of Robert

Moses. Moses at one time simultaneously held twelve separate city and state positions in New York and became the "boss" through whom almost all important decisions and job appointments had to pass. Marrow, in moral indignation, denounced Moses' style: "In evaluation of his leadership, we must consider the homes he destroyed, the lives he ruined, the neighborhoods he bulldozed, the humiliations he piled on subordinates, the careers he crushed, the hundreds of millions of dollars he wasted—how he brutalized the poor and appeased the powerful." And then he added, "Apparently, Moses was able to blind himself to all this. He could ignore his own self-centered motivations and publicly speak of his devotions to the democratic process and the power of the people to be the ultimate decision makers. But he never recognized the gap between creed and deed" (Caro, 1975, p. 39).

Marrow summarized his talk at Hawthorne by drawing some implications for modern management: "The daily nervous and mental frustrations that our workers experience also take a serious toll on their health, and that means in the aggregate, the national health. Such psychosomatic illnesses also add to the general inefficiency and excessive cost of our industrial production. Rising absenteeism from the job, malingering and vandalism are alarming symptoms of the psychological malaise that is spreading everywhere in our country. Work must provide a more attractive lure. It must offer mental stimulation, challenge and a lift to personal morale which it is inherently quite able to do. . . . Now, as never before, the most promising option is a scientific yet humanistic approach with a passionate concern by leaders to release to the full, the latent talents and energies of the people they direct so that employees will work at their best and productivity will increase" (Marrow, 1975, pp. 47–48).

The behavioral style, as we can see, is people oriented and exhibits a keen sensitivity on directed, personal feelings. People with this style tend to be empathetic and to accord worth and compassion to those with whom they work. *Love* is the word that best summarizes their caring for other people. They agree with James Hillman that "Loving is a way of knowing, and

for loving to know, it must personify. Personifying is thus a way
of knowing, especially knowing what is invisibly hidden in the
heart" (Hillman, 1975, p. 15).

The inclination of those with the behavioral style to personify permeates everything they do. They are good listeners—
attentive to the individual—and good communicators. They
prefer the "soft" data of personal experience over the so-called
"hard" data of questionnaires, statistical calculations, and
detached analyses. It is through direct personal experience that
they come to know and to understand; they prefer face-to-face
meetings and discussions to reports and memorandums. Their
management style is to engage people on an individual basis
and to look for solutions that are consistent with each person's
values and goals by muting the conflict between differing personalities. They try to be as supportive and empathetic to each
individual as possible. Because they devote so much of their attention and emotions to each individual, executives with the
behavioral style find it difficult to manage and direct large groups
of people under conditions—such as war—that call for a high
degree of efficiency and authority.

Harold Geneen: The Directive Style

Harold Geneen, like Robert Moses and General Patton,
typifies the person with a dominant directive style. He focused
on short-term results and strove—indeed, strained—to maintain absolute control of every activity with which he was involved. This drive and commitment are also responsible for one
of the great success stories in corporate history.

Geneen began his career as an accountant with Lybrand,
Ross Brothers and Montgomery. After about eight years of
auditing and advising others, he decided that he wanted to control a business himself and accepted an executive position with
American Can. He succeeded in that job and soon held a series
of senior positions at Bell and Howell, Jones and Laughlin Steel,
and Ratheon. These jobs were all pretenders to the throne and
not the top job, and so he turned to an executive recruiting service and asked them to find him a CEO position, one in which
he could forge the direction of the company to his own liking.

The recruiters found the perfect spot at ITT. The company had been meandering purposelessly since the death of its popular leader, Sosthenes Behn, and needed a clear sense of direction and firm guiding hand. Consultants had recommended that ITT needed a strong, decisive, authoritarian leader. That kind of position was just what Geneen wanted. As he put it, he hated to "gamble on what other people did." He wanted control of his own destiny. So in May 1959, when he was offered the job, he jumped at it.

Geneen's initial success was phenomenal. ITT's gross annual profit grew from about $8 hundred million to about $11 billion during the first twelve years of his reign. By 1980, ITT owned more than 250 companies and grossed $22 billion a year. It was the paragon of a growth company, with an earnings-per-share growth rate in excess of 10 percent per quarter for fifty-one consecutive quarters. Much of this success was due to his unbounded energy, his decisiveness, his exceptional attention to technical detail, his mania for cost savings—during Geneen's days as a corporate finance officer, one colleague described him as "a bloodhound on the trail of a wasted dollar"—and, above all, his ability to retain total control of the corporation.

Geneen's insatiable appetite for control was fed by carloads of facts, which showed that he also had a strong analytical style. He always kept between fifteen and twenty attaché cases piled behind his desk—one for each of the divisions or problem areas he was dealing with. They were constantly filled and refilled with the flood of paperwork that flowed continuously from ITT's worldwide operations. Under Geneen, ITT grew to a point where it operated in every country in the free world. Wherever he went, whether at home at night, on business trips to Europe, or on weekend vacations at his cottage in New England, he took several of these briefcases with him. Their contents were the instigator of many a wee-hour phone call to a company or division manager inquiring as to why a sales quota had not been met or why there was an unexplained variance in a cost budget.

Warren Bennis, in a review of Robert Schoenberg's biography of Geneen, shows how this thirst for facts affected his entire philosophy of management:

The impression we get of Geneen the man is that
of a person totally consumed with the hegemony
of facts. He once wrote a memo that stated: "Facts:
the highest art of professional management . . . requires the temerity, intellectual curiosity, guts and/
or plain impoliteness, if necessary, to be sure that
what you do have is indeed to have what we will
call an 'unshakeable fact.'"

      According to Schoenberg, "Facts, not peo-
ple, made decisions at ITT." As one treads through
the treacherous corporate waters with Geneen, two
strong impressions emerge: First, Geneen acted on
the belief that people were malleable objects that
were interchangeable and could be manipulated
while facts were unshakeable and hence, real.
"And, second . . . more important than that impression though related to it, is what leadership is
all about . . . . Geneen is the archetypal manager
interested in efficiency rather than effectiveness,
depersonalizing and rationalizing human behavior
instead of cultivating and developing it." He was
a manager who sought to do things right away, not
a leader who was dedicated to doing the right thing
[Bennis, 1985, p. 9].

This scrupulous respect for life in the concrete and refusal to
bend fact to fit thesis is typical of the directive style. It is important to note that the analytical style, which Geneen also used,
tends to rely heavily on facts because of a technical orientation
and emphasis on rumination and calculation. Each of these two
styles, however, views facts in a different way. The analytical
style seeks facts to fit into a priori mental models, because,
philosophically, the analytical person is a rationalist. A rationalist
acquires facts in order to verify beliefs derived from intuition
and thinking. The directive style, on the other hand, resembles
the style of the empiricist school. Facts for the directive style
are reality, and there is a commensurate distaste for ideology.
The person with the directive style believes that it is through

the accumulation of and dealing with facts that true knowledge is acquired. Facts also serve as a kind of security blanket for the person with the directive style, assuaging the intense need for mastery and control.

Witness Williamson's quotations from Patton:

"We have men's lives hanging on our decisions! We cannot assume anything. Whether we are in the desert or actual combat we must get the facts. How are you going to feel when you make a decision and several hundred men are killed? You want to try assuming that they are not dead? Never forget, colonel, that the life you save may be your own!"

General Patton wanted exact facts about everything involving an operation. He wanted the exact weight of a gallon of gas, hot and cold! He wanted his staff to know in seconds the number of gallons an Armored Division would require in order to move fifty miles. He wanted the exact weight of rations for one day, ten days, and any number of days he requested. General Patton said, "Let's never have to look at each other and say, 'If only we had known!' We will always know" [Williamson, 1979, p. 123].

The technical and factual orientation of the directive and analytical styles keeps them from being very people oriented (the behavioral and conceptual styles tend to have the deepest concern for people), and this shows up in their management style as well. Psychologists explain that Patton's actions failed to protect the egos of the men he commanded. Geneen, too, suffered this criticism. He was intense. This would often manifest itself, as it did with Patton, in colorful language, mispronunciations, and mixed metaphors: "I believe in pushing and pulling and kneading and whittling until I get two purple drops" (Williamson, 1979, p. 26). He also demanded equally high levels of intensity from those who worked for him. One would have to be eager, ambitious, energetic, and, indeed, very self-confident to work for Geneen. He frequently called meetings that lasted as long as four days and nights—an in-house publication once spoofed these marathon meetings by showing a photograph of Geneen in a cartoon saying, "Good morning, Gentlemen! . . . We'll break for dinner at midnight" (Williamson, 1979, p. 123).

This intensity and demand for total involvement and commitment from his associates had their costs. Many of his executives "burned out." Among those who quit or were fired, quite a few, having learned their lesson at "Geneen U.," went on to become presidents of other major firms. Among the "alumni" are George Strichman, Neil Firestone, William Duke, John Lobb, and Henry Bowes. Geneen focused on matters that could be captured by numbers and left the people activities to others, such as Jack Hanway, a senior executive at ITT who worked closely with Geneen and from whom he demanded full loyalty. These others were given the unpleasant tasks of firing and reprimanding. Geneen prided himself on his "realistic impersonal" decisions. This, of course, led to an inability to relate to humans.

Geneen's style while he was at ITT is typical of the directive. He was focused, quick moving, results oriented, and generally effective in achieving his goals. He liked power, status, and tangible rewards as measures of success—Geneen made $767,000 a year at ITT and claimed that he was worth "maybe" $5 million. Using his analytical style, he relied heavily on his ability to take in data from the outside world in the form of specific facts and technical detail as a basis for making decisions. As a directive, he sought structure in his work. Geneen emphasized speed and action in everything he did and surrounded himself with people who were energetic, ambitious, and loyal, people who would carry out his orders as he issued them. Most of all, however, Geneen sought control over his far-flung enterprises. As *Business Week* put it, Geneen was the "undisputed monarch of the 'Sovereign State of ITT.' . . . Geneen and the company are inseparable" ("The Sovereign State of ITT," 1973, p. 102).

Most of us in our daily lives use some backup styles in addition to our dominant styles. We are analytical when we study things carefully, conceptual when we create new ideas, behavioral when we engage in an intense relationship with another individual, and directive when we move into action to get things done. A truly flexible personality is one with a capacity in each of these pure styles. Generally, what we have found is that a person tends to prefer one or two of these pure decision styles over the others. That is, in the absence of constraints, a person will stress one or more of these stylistic categories to the exclusion of the others.

The four archetypes described in this chapter were chosen, as was the contrast between Patton and Bradley, because they are representative of people in highly visible positions of leadership who used one particular style extensively. Our intent was to provide substance and a point of reference to the concept of the four basic styles. These are fundamental to the development of complex style patterns, which will be described later in the book. They also form the basic units in the language of decision style.

Our data show that few people exclusively exhibit just one of these pure decision styles. For example, we have identified sixteen "basic" patterns of style and 156 overall patterns. Our studies show that a typical person has one or two "dominant" styles—that is, he or she scores well above the average for those styles on the Decision Style Inventory. We also find that most people have one or two "backup," or supporting, styles as well. The archetypes described in this chapter also exhibit multiple styles with various levels of dominance. McNamara, for example, clearly had a directive and conceptual backup to his analytical style. Land certainly was analytical when he brought his scientific thinking to bear on conceptual ideas. His personnel policies also demonstrate a backup behavioral style. Marrow, a scholar, theorist, and researcher, had a strong conceptual style to back up his behavioral style. Indeed, Marrow's case presents an interesting example of the psychic tensions that build up within people because of the competing demands placed on them by different components of their style.

As one with a behavioral style, Marrow tended to particularize; that is, to deal with people as individuals, much the same way as a novelist does or as Anton Checkov does in his plays. Yet, as a theorist, he sought to speak about humanity as a whole, and herein lay the dilemma. In practicing the scientific method and using his conceptual and analytical skills, he could say nothing about a person as an individual, except as to how that person related to other people. Nonetheless, it was his ability to synthesize among these competing demands that made him an exceptional leader. This characteristic of balancing competing demands typifies successful people. They are able to reconcile differences in their styles and achieve the best that each has to offer. Many chief executive officers whom we have interviewed have both a conceptual style—for planning and innovation—and a directive style—for deciding and directing. Alan Zakon, chief executive officer of the Boston Consulting Group, postulates that to exploit new opportunities, management style (which reflects an individual's decision style) will be "far more important than the structure of the organization" (Zakon, 1983, p. 10). These findings will be expanded in later chapters.

The four basic styles we have presented provide a conceptual framework for classifying the way people think and decide. They give meaning to the differences in behavior that we observe in everyday life. To make these concepts useful as a management tool, we will extend them so that they provide insight into individual behavior. The Decision Style Inventory was developed as a means to measure style. Ideally, such an instrument should be easy to administer, economical, compatible with the person's mind-set, and yet accurate in its classification. The Decision Style Inventory is an instrument that meets these requirements. It brings specificity to the language of decision style and permits discussions on style to proceed from a basis of data. The next chapter describes the DSI and how it can be applied both for personal use and for achieving success as an executive.

3

●ΙΙ●ΙΙ●ΙΙ●ΙΙ●ΙΙ●ΙΙ●ΙΙ●ΙΙ●ΙΙ●ΙΙ●ΙΙ●ΙΙ●ΙΙ●ΙΙ●ΙΙ●ΙΙ●ΙΙ●ΙΙ●ΙΙ●ΙΙ●ΙΙ●ΙΙ●ΙΙ●ΙΙ●ΙΙ●ΙΙ●ΙΙ●ΙΙ●ΙΙ●ΙΙ●

How to Measure Style:
Using the Decision Style Inventory

Unless knowledge can be measured and expressed in numerical form or rank, it is meager and often unsatisfactory or inconclusive. "Meager" is the way to describe our knowledge about our own and others' styles. Communicating ideas effectively requires a measure of comparability. In developing a language, one can either rely primarily on abstract concepts or utilize the power of numerical representation, which gives relative measures of the factors under consideration. In designing the Decision Style Inventory, we chose to rely on numerical values, so that one individual could be compared with another on a sounder basis than the generalities that are often used. Managers tend to prefer a tool that can be used in an unbiased manner and that has good predictive capability. Here again, numerical values are superior to a more descriptive approach.

The Decision Style Inventory has been used by well over 10,000 individuals, including presidents of companies, board chairs, corporate planners, architects, chiefs of police, army generals, nurses, teachers, and so on. It has shown excellent face validity in that well over 90 percent of the people who take the inventory agree with its findings. It also is able to predict with considerable accuracy the careers that one would find meaningful. The results of a detail validation study are shown in Appendix A.

Because of the large number of people who have taken the inventory and because of its reliability, you can feel confident that the scores you obtain can be used to determine your style. Results of a number of different studies are described as examples throughout this book, and sample data for senior executives and for entrepreneurs are shown in Appendixes B and C. Taking the inventory yourself and computing your scores will help you to understand the meaning of style and how it applies directly to yourself, as well as to the examples given in this book.

In a sense, the Decision Style Inventory works very much like a prism. It takes your responses to the questions and reflects them through a spectrum that separates them into four basic decision styles: directive, analytical, conceptual, and behavioral. Your scores on the Decision Style Inventory reveal where you fit in the spectrum as compared with others who have taken the test. You can examine degree of dominance of each of the four styles, which shows the intensity of your preference for each style. You will be able to use this information to determine the alignment between your style and your present or proposed occupation. The data have been arranged so that they are statistically easy to apply and interpret. For example, if your score falls within the normal range, which we call backup, it means that it is similar to that of 38 percent of all the people we have surveyed. We will discuss the interpretation and application of your scores later in this chapter; for now, we will look more closely at the instrument itself and explain how it is administered and scored.

Using the Decision Style Inventory

The Decision Style Inventory, shown in Figure 1, consists of twenty questions, each with four responses, that concern typical situations facing executives. Although each of the four responses to a particular question may appear equally desirable or undesirable, the instrument is designed to force individuals to "rank," or differentiate among, them. There are no "right" or "wrong" answers; the scores reflect your preferences for the different responses. In the scoring approach that we have employed, each response is ranked either 1, 2, 4, or 8, with the highest number indicating the greatest degree of preference; thus, a ranking of 1 indicates the response that you least prefer, 2 indicates a response that you consider on occasion, 4 indicates a response that you consider often, and 8 indicates the response that you most prefer. (Through extensive experimentation, we have found that doubling, rather than merely increasing by one, the score for each succeeding level of preference results in a more accurate measurement than does ranking the responses 1 through 4.) Each response in any set of four must be ranked differently; though two responses within a given set may seem equally preferable, you must choose one that you feel better represents your preference.

As you respond to the questions, think about how you typically make decisions in your work situation. Your responses should reflect how *you* feel about the questions and what *you* prefer to do, not what you believe is correct or desirable. Some people find it easier to first choose their most and least preferred responses, and then to rank the remaining two; the order in which you answer is not important, so long as you rank each response. There is no time limit for completing the inventory.

Once all of the responses have been ranked, the scores in each column are totaled. The total score for column one represents the directive style, column two the analytical style, column three the conceptual style, and column four the behavioral style. These total scores can then be compared with those of others who have completed the inventory. The typical scores for each style are: directive—75; analytical—90; conceptual—80; and behavioral—55. Differences in your scores from the typical scores can be explained by intensity, or style dominance. We have found that the level of dominance resembles a bell-shaped curve. This regularity allows us to make statements regarding an individual's preference for a given style. A measure of variability called the standard deviation is used to identify the levels of intensity or dominance for each style.

The bell-shaped curve with the typical (or average) scores for the directive style is shown in Figure 2. For example, 38 percent of the scores fall in the range of half a standard deviation on either side of the average. Because the average is the score that is typical for most people, the range around the

Figure 1. Decision Style Inventory.

1. My prime objective is to:	Have a position with status	Be the best in my field	Achieve recognition for my work	Feel secure in my job
2. I enjoy jobs that:	Are technical and well defined	Have considerable variety	Allow independent action	Involve people
3. I expect people working for me to be:	Productive and fast	Highly capable	Committed and responsive	Receptive to suggestions
4. In my job, I look for:	Practical results	The best solutions	New approaches or ideas	Good working environment
5. I communicate best with others:	On a direct one-to-one basis	In writing	By having a group discussion	In a formal meeting
6. In my planning I emphasize:	Current problems	Meeting objectives	Future goals	Developing people's careers
7. When faced with solving a problem, I:	Rely on proven approaches	Apply careful analysis	Look for creative approaches	Rely on my feelings
8. When using information, I prefer:	Specific facts	Accurate and complete data	Broad coverage of many options	Limited data that are easily understood
9. When I am not sure about what to do, I:	Rely on intuition	Search for facts	Look for a possible compromise	Wait before making a decision
10. Whenever possible, I avoid:	Long debates	Incomplete work	Using numbers or formulas	Conflict with others

11. I am especially good at:	Remembering dates and facts	Solving difficult problems	Seeing many possibilities	Interacting with others
12. When time is important, I:	Decide and act quickly	Follow plans and priorities	Refuse to be pressured	Seek guidance or support
13. In social settings, I generally:	Speak with others	Think about what is being said	Observe what is going on	Listen to the conversation
14. I am good at remembering:	People's names	Places we met	People's faces	People's personalities
15. The work I do provides me:	The power to influence others	Challenging assignments	Achieving my personal goals	Acceptance by the group
16. I work well with those who are:	Energetic and ambitious	Self-confident	Open-minded	Polite and trusting
17. When under stress, I:	Become anxious	Concentrate on the problem	Become frustrated	Am forgetful
18. Others consider me:	Aggressive	Disciplined	Imaginative	Supportive
19. My decisions typically are:	Realistic and direct	Systematic or abstract	Broad and flexible	Sensitive to the needs of others
20. I dislike:	Losing control	Boring work	Following rules	Being rejected

average is called "backup" style. The next grouping is for the "dominant" category, which has 15 percent of the population. The "very dominant" category represents 16 percent of the population. Thus, 69 percent of the scores will fall into one of these three levels of intensity; and the remaining 31 percent are considered as "least preferred," or the category where the style is seldom used.

Figure 2. Degrees of Dominance for the Directive Style.

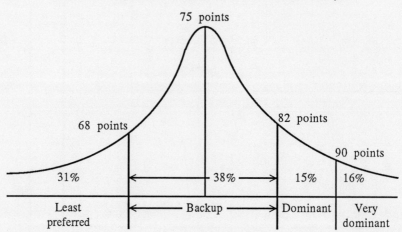

To illustrate how to interpret the level of dominance, we will rely on the standard deviation. Our data showed that the standard deviation (the measure used to determine how much variability there is) was approximately 15. To simplify interpretation, we used 15 as the measure of variability for each of the four styles. Starting with the directive style, the typical score is 75 and standard deviation is 15. This is our operational definition of a "typical" person—that is, one whose score is the average of the population. Next, we will show how to determine the level of intensity or dominance. First, we will refer to the following definitions:

1. *Least preferred.* This is the style that is seldom used. If the score is more than 7 points (approximately half of the standard deviation) below the average, then we call this "least

preferred." Only 31 percent of the people score in this category, while 69 percent have higher scores. For example, if your directive score is 59, then it is 16 points below the average of 75 and is least preferred.

2. *Backup.* This is one that you would use when the occasion demanded. If your score is either 7 points above or below the average, your style intensity would be in the backup category. Approximately 38 percent of the people score in this category, 31 percent score lower, and 31 percent score higher. For example, for the analytical style, the average score is 90, and the backup score falls between 83 and 97, which is a half a standard deviation on either side of the typical or average score. If your score were 86, this would be a backup style for you.

3. *Dominant.* A person whose score is in this category will use this style frequently. To be in this category, the score must be at least 7 points but no more than 15 points above the average. About 15 percent of the people score in this category in one or more of their styles. For example, the conceptual style has an average or typical score of 80. For a person whose score for the conceptual style is 89 (between 87 and 95), that style is dominant.

4. *Very dominant.* This refers to scores that are more than 15 points above the average. For example, a score of 74 for the behavioral style is 19 points above the average of 55, indicating that this style is very dominant. Approximately 16 percent of the people have a very dominant style category in any of the four styles. If your score for a particular style were in this category, that style would be used almost exclusively in most situations.

We have summarized these scores for the "typical" individual in Table 1.

An Illustrative Example

Fran Chandler, a busy chief executive officer, will be used to describe how to interpret decision style scores. A successful

Table 1. Typical Range of Style Scores.

	Least Preferred	Backup	Dominant	Very Dominant
Directive	20 to 67	68 to 81	82 to 89	90 to 160
Analytical	20 to 82	83 to 96	97 to 104	105 to 160
Conceptual	20 to 72	73 to 86	87 to 94	95 to 160
Behavioral	20 to 47	48 to 61	62 to 69	70 to 160

president of two corporations, mother of two daughters, wife, teacher, and consultant, Chandler grew up in a rural area, and her family moved several times before she entered high school. She was the second of four children, with an elder brother. Free expression and competing for good grades were emphasized during her upbringing. Chandler has taught in the Business School at California State University. She has a sense of humor, feels that business is fun, and is a good communicator. She dislikes losing control and wants to run the show. Her decision style is one of the typical patterns that we have found for senior executives. She is highly analytical and conceptual; her decision style scores are shown in Figure 3.

Figure 3. Example of Decision Style Scores.

Analytical 92 (backup)	Conceptual 91 (dominant)	183 (ideas)
Directive 68 (backup)	Behavioral 49 (backup)	117 (action)
160 (left brain)	140 (right brain)	300

Chandler's dominant conceptual score reflects her preference for visualizing future possibilities, formulating new options for her businesses, and identifying creative solutions for problems confronting the companies. Her three backup scores show a very flexible person who is able to use any of the other three styles when needed. Thus, she can be forceful and results oriented (directive), or she can be logical and careful about choosing alternatives (analytical), and she can be empathetic and understanding when the situation requires it (behavioral).

What does this example tell you about style? To start, because Chandler's directive score is in the range of 68 to 82, it is a backup style that would often be used when needed or when she is under stress. The behavioral and analytical scores are also in the backup category, which signifies that she would use these styles only when needed. Finally, the fact that her conceptual score is in the dominant category suggests that she would use this style most frequently and that she is a very creative person with a broad perspective who has the vision to see future alternatives. Because style is innate, we do not think about which style we are going to use in each decision situation. Rather, we behave in a manner that tends to be consistent with our style. Thus, Chandler's decisions reflect her style and influence her behavior.

The Basic Styles

The key characteristics of the basic styles will be described to provide a basis for interpreting your score. Using Fran Chandler as our example, we will show what the individual scores mean.

Directive. This style is characterized by its practical orientation and its emphasis on the "here and now." People with this style tend to use data that focus on specific facts and to prefer structure. They are action oriented and decisive and look for speed, efficiency, and results. People with this style can be autocratic and exercise power and control. Their focus is short range, and they tend to have the drive and energy needed to accomplish difficult tasks. They also focus on problems internal to the organization. Interestingly, they sometimes feel insecure and want status to protect their position. Because Chandler's score of 68 is in the backup category for this style, it is not used as frequently as her dominant style. She would typically avoid using power or being autocratic to achieve her goals. Following is a summary of the characteristics of this style.

Psychological aspects

Focuses on	Tasks and technical problems
Considers	Facts, rules, and procedures
Acquires information	By sensing and using short reports with limited data
Evaluates information	Using intuition, experience, or rules
Complexity	Has a low tolerance for ambiguity and needs structure

Leadership style

Characteristics	Is practical, matter of fact, authoritarian
Social orientation	Is impersonal; needs power and status; is forceful; dislikes committees and group discussions
Task orientation	Is quick; is action and results oriented
Motivation	Situations with measurable achievement potential, tangible rewards

Best organizational fit	Structured, goal-oriented, such as bureaucracies, or where power and authority are important
Major criticism	Too rigid, impersonal, simplistic, autocratic

Analytical. This style is characterized by the tendency to over-analyze a situation or to always search for the best possible solution. Because Chandler's score for this style (92) is also backup, she would periodically enjoy solving problems, searching for complete and accurate facts, and carefully studying the facts to see what possibilities exist when this is important. People with this style often reach top posts in their companies, and while very technical in their outlook, they can often be autocratic. This style responds well to new requirements. Chandler displays a number of the characteristics typical of this style. She wants to be considered the best person in her field, and she enjoys challenging assignments with considerable variety. Generally, she is good at detail planning when she has to do it. When she uses her analytical style extensively, some people consider her a little too disciplined and precise and feel that it takes her forever to make a decision. This style may be summarized as follows:

Psychological aspects

Focuses on	Tasks and technical problems involving a logical approach
Considers	Every aspect of a given problem
Acquires information	By careful analysis, using a large number of data
Evaluates information	Through abstract thinking, avoiding incomplete data
Complexity	High tolerance for ambiguity, innovative in solving problems

Leadership style

Characteristics	Intellectual, ingenious, wants control
Social orientation	Impersonal, skilled in organizing facts, establishes controls, prefers limited control by others
Task orientation	Applies rigorous analysis, prepares elaborate, detailed plans
Motivation	Enjoys complex situations with variety and challenge, wants to be able to predict outcomes

Best organizational fit	Impersonal, planning, solving complex problems, science, engineering, and so on
Major criticism	Too dogmatic, overcontrolling, impersonal, careful, abstract or mathematical; sometimes too slow

Conceptual. This style, on which Chandler's score is 91, is characterized by creativity and a broad outlook, although she may rely too much on intuition and feelings. She is good at getting along with others, enjoys having discussions, and is willing to compromise. She is curious and open-minded but wants independence and dislikes following rules. Conceptual executives are perfectionists, want to see many options, and are concerned about the future. They tend to be creative in finding answers to problems and can easily visualize alternatives and consequences. They tend to closely associate with their organization and value praise, recognition, and independence. They prefer loose control and are willing to share power. This is Chandler's dominant style; consequently, she will use it frequently. This explains why she is considered very imaginative. On occasion, however, some people consider her to be a dreamer. This style is summarized below:

Psychological aspects

Focuses on	People and broad aspects of a problem
Considers	Many options and future possibilities
Acquires information	By using intuition and discussion with others
Evaluates information	By integrating diverse cues to reach conclusions, applying judgement
Complexity	High tolerance for ambiguity; takes risks and is very creative

Leadership style

Characteristic	Is insightful and enthusiastic
Social orientation	Very personal, shows concern for others' views, smooths over difficulties, is well liked
Task orientation	Is adaptive and flexible, uses intuition, seeks new ideas
Motivation	Seeks recognition from others, wants independence, enjoys achieving personal goals

Best organizational fit — Loose, decentralized settings, open or organic organization

Major criticism — Is a dilettante; too idealistic, "indecisive," imaginative, slow, difficult to control

Behavioral. This style is the one that is most people-oriented of all four. Chandler's score in this category, 49, is in the backup range. She enjoys being involved with people and exchanging views with them. She is a good listener and is interested in others. Executives with this style also are very supportive, are receptive to suggestions, show warmth, use persuasion, accept loose control, and prefer verbal to written reports. They tend to focus on short-run problems and are action oriented. This style is typical of individuals who want acceptance and who are willing to share with others. The behavioral style is summarized below:

Psychological aspects

Focuses on	People, social aspects of the work situation
Considers	Feelings, well-being of others
Acquires information	By sensing, listening, and interacting with others
Evaluates information	Using feelings; instincts
Complexity	Has a low tolerance for ambiguity

Leadership style

Characteristics	Sociable, friendly, supportive
Social orientation	Talent for building teams, encourages participation
Task orientation	Is action oriented, holds meetings
Motivation	Acceptance by peers, avoidance of conflict
Best organizational fit	Well-designed, people-oriented, collegial settings
Major criticism	Too concerned about others; too "wishy-washy," sensitive, can't make hard decisions, can't say no

Style Patterns

Figure 3 also shows Fran Chandler's style patterns, which represent combinations of style. Although her dominant style is conceptual, she is quite comfortable in using the other three styles—her backup styles. Most people have multiple styles and are able to use these in ways that show their preferences in given circumstances.

To understand style patterns, why not try to find your own? In addition to the score for each of the four basic styles, compute your combined scores. As we will see, some of the patterns have significance for other purposes. For example, the combined analytical and directive scores reflect our left brain orientation—a strong technical focus and an inclination to logical thinking. The combined conceptual and behavioral scores, on the other hand, reflect right brain orientation—a strong concern for people, broad thinking, and creativity. Can someone have both a left and a right brain orientation? The answer is definitely yes. We have found that most successful executives exhibit both left and right brain styles. This is certainly true for Fran Chandler, who has at least a backup score for the styles that reflect each brainsidedness. For example, her right brain orientation has a score of 140, which is higher than the average person's score of 135 for the two styles on the right side.

If we examine Chandler's combined analytical and conceptual scores, we see that she is oriented to thinking and ideas. In contrast, the person who has high combined directive and behavioral scores tends to be action oriented and to enjoy dealing with people. As with left and right brain, a person can be both thinking and action oriented. For example, according to the results of a number of studies that we have done, entrepreneurs tend to have high conceptual and high directive scores. This combination reflects their ability to visualize opportunities and then be able to bring them to fruition because of their results orientation. Chandler's combined conceptual and directive score of 159 is higher than the typical score of 155, which indicates that she has an entrepreneurial bent.

A summary of what we term "basic patterns" that are combinations of pure styles are shown in Table 2. The patterns shown in Table 2 are only 7 out of 256 possible patterns. To examine this large number of combinations of style, we have employed a computer program that matches the patterns with suggested careers (Rowe and Cox, 1986). The results have shown a high correlation between style and job preference.

To explain the meaning of combined scores, we will return to Fran Chandler's scores. Her combined conceptual and behavioral score of 140 shows a right brain or people orientation. In addition, her dominant conceptual score places her in the right brain category. Her combined analytical and conceptual score is 183, which places her in the thinking or ideas category. However, the fact that her combined directive and behavioral score is below 130 suggests that she generally thinks before she takes any action. To summarize the meaning of Chandler's scores, we can say that she is dominant conceptual with a balance of backup scores in the other three styles. She is definitely more thinking than action oriented, and she favors dealing with people rather than numbers. Because her combined conceptual and analytical score is 159 (which is higher than the typical 155), she would fit the executive mode of management. As would be expected, the typical job that would fit this pattern of styles is

Table 2. Basic Style Patterns.

Pattern	Score	Typical of
Left brain (analytical + directive)	165 or higher	Science, finance, law
Right brain (conceptual + behavioral)	135 or higher	Psychology, teachers, artists
Idea orientation (analytical + conceptual)	170 or higher	Senior executives, leaders
Action orientation (directive + behavioral)	130 or higher	Supervisors, sales people, athletes
Executive (conceptual + directive)	155 or higher	Entrepreneurs, crossover executives
Staff (analytical + behavioral)	145 or higher	Technical managers
Middle management (directive + analytical + conceptual)	245 or higher	Flexible management style

that of senior executive. However, Chandler would also enjoy working as an architect, professor, consultant, lawyer, or staff person. Thus, we see that there is not a one-for-one match between style and job; rather, there are a number of possible careers that a person with Chandler's style could pursue.

Conclusion

While we can generalize on how to interpret Decision Style Inventory scores, many other factors contribute to success in an organizational setting. An individual's decision is influenced by his or her values, as well as by the context in which the decision is made, its urgency, the time available, resources needed, and so on. Moreover, styles are complex. Their interpretation, application, and usefulness require an understanding that goes beyond the mere mechanics of how to score the Decision Style Inventory. Nevertheless, the inventory provides a window into why and how people think and act. To the person who pursues the study of style, this can be extremely valuable information on how to manage more effectively. In studying real decision makers, we have observed the closeness between what they actually do and what we might expect on the basis of their styles. It is this correlation between observation and style that has propelled our studies to include many different organizations and a variety of career requirements. We have also studied many interesting executives whose decisions often determine the success of their companies.

Now that you have completed the Decision Style Inventory and determined your own style, you can compare yourself with the people described in this book and be on the road to becoming proficient in using the language of style. The next chapter will help you gain an appreciation of the concepts and the background that led to the development of the Decision Style Inventory.

4

●‖●

Development and Utility
of the Decision Style Inventory:
Aligning Decisions and Context

"The great decisions of human life, as a rule, have far more to do with instincts and other mysterious unconscious factors than with conscious will and well-meaning reasonableness. The shoe that fits one person pinches another. There is no recipe for living that suits all cases" (Johnson, 1979, p. 3). The differences described in this quotation from Jung form a basic theme underlying decision styles. While individual differences in style are elusive, a better understanding of them is valuable, both for aligning people with appropriate careers and for helping them meet the demands placed upon them.

The real world of an organization is to a large extent determined by an individual's "frame of reference." Elbing describes the concept of self-awareness succinctly by stating that "to understand the infinite data in an organization, the decision maker must first have an accurate insight in his or her frame of reference that structures [the] world" (Elbing, 1970, p. 171). To manage successfully, then, one should know and accept feelings, sensitivities, values, and style.

Frames of reference provide us with guides and insight into understanding the complexity of human thinking and decision making. How can we plumb the depths of people's feelings, preferences, and thought processes? Answers to questions such as this are not easy. Often, one frame of reference begets another, and we find that the cross fertilization that relates one field of study to another can introduce new concepts, perspectives, and frameworks on which to build meaningful approaches. A number of the basic concepts used in the development of our approach to decision styles integrated frames or structures from social psychology, cognitive psychology, organization behavior, management, information systems, and structural engineering. For example, a basic frame or model that we will describe combines concepts of equilibrium in the analysis of engineering structures with work done in the field of social psychology that analyzed factors that affect human behavior.

The Decision Style Model

The decision style model in Figure 4 shows what characteristics are associated with each of the four basic styles. On the left axis, it shows the distinction between high cognitive complexity—thinking orientation—and its counterpart, low cognitive complexity—action orientation. Thus, Figure 4 illustrates that there are thinkers and there are doers. This interpretation is consistent with Zaleznick's (1977) dichotomy between the leader who uses ideas to deal proactively with the future and the manager who reacts to situations to improve current performance. At the bottom of Figure 4, the task and people orientations reflect personal values that we all hold to be sacrosanct. This dichotomy is consistent with approaches that focus on the technical or behavioral concerns of managers. However, these approaches do not consider cognitive complexity in their formulation.

The initial approach to measuring style evolved out of work done by Rowe (1974b) that dealt with understanding the environmental forces that impinge on a decision maker. The next phase in the development of the inventory was an early version of the test used to study navy leadership (Rowe, Weingart, and Provenzano, 1977).

The early work of Kurt Lewin revealed that the environment had a profound effect on how people respond to demands placed on them. Lewin, an emigré social psychologist, often used a simple exercise to help people in trying situations. On a sheet

Figure 4. Decision Style Model.

	Analytical	*Conceptual*	
Thinking orientation	Control Logic Variety	Achievement Systems Creative	Leader Proactive Adaptive
	Directive	*Behavioral*	
Action orientation	Power Structure Speed	Support Persuasion Empathy	Manager Reactive Rules
	Task orientation	People orientation	

of paper, he would draw a vertical line to represent their problem. He then would ask them to draw on one side an arrow for every force that could support them and on the other side an arrow for every force that worked against them and thus resisted their progress. Then he would have them examine the balance between these two sets of forces and help them devise a strategy for coping with the problem areas. Using this crude but effective application of field force analysis, he was able to help many people find a more effective alignment. In doing this, he noted that the forces tended to come from four principal sources: the individual him- or herself, the task before him or her, the group that he or she was a part of, and the outside environment. Rowe's formulation extended Lewin's work by adding a requirement for equilibrium. His Four Force Model was an adaptation of the principle that all physical structures, in order to remain in "equilibrium," must have all four forces in balance.

These four forces were used as the basis for developing the questions for the test instrument. Figure 5 examines the way individuals respond to the four forces. The first force represents our *personal needs*—the wants, desires, motivation, and drives that propel us in every situation we face. Next is the *task*—the specific requirements of the job that must be done and the nature of the work situation. The *group* is the organization and the people with whom we interact, exerting pressure for conformity. Finally, we have the *environment*—that set of external factors that

Figure 5. The Four Force Model.

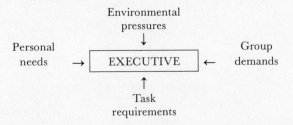

influence what we do but over which we have little or no control. This factor includes the overall company and such external factors as unions.

When we respond to each of the four forces, we have a tendency to behave in a rather habitual way. The manner of response is strongly influenced by our decision style. Thus, if we know people's styles, we can often predict how they will behave in situations that they encounter and are able to recommend what action can be used to compensate for a least preferred style and to understand which situations to avoid.

The Bicameral Brain

Recent research has added to our understanding of the neurological basis of decision style and hence establishes a scientific foundation for determining one's match to the job. The brain has been found to be bicameral, consisting of a left and a right hemisphere. Decision styles reflect the fact that thinking can be described as either primarily "left brain"—logical/deductive—or "right brain"—relational/spatial/inductive. People who evidence either analytical or directive styles tend to focus on work and to be concerned with tangible results. This type of thinking uses the left side of the brain. In counterdistinction, those who are either conceptual or behavioral tend to be more concerned about people, ideas, creativity, and visualizing. These are all activities usually associated with the right side of the brain.

The precise mechanism by which the brain receives, stores, and retrieves information is not fully understood; however, we do know that only a very small percentage of our

our brain cells are ever utilized. The implication is that our propensity for knowledge acquisition is far greater than we would expect. The use of knowledge in the cognitive process appears to be governed by specific areas in the brain and does not appear to be susceptible to change.

Environmental Propensity

Our ability to respond to environmental forces is termed "environmental propensity." This identifies one's predisposition to focus on one aspect of the environment to the exclusion of others. Some people have a tendency to focus on the more objective aspects of their environment, which we have called the task or technical orientation, while others have a tendency to deal more with the subjective aspects of their environment, which we have called the people, social, or organizational orientation.

An individual who has a high level of environmental propensity—that is, whose predispositions match the demands of his or her environment—can readily accommodate to the environment, develops a higher commitment to the work to be performed, forms a better understanding of others, is willing to compromise and meet work expectations, and has high levels of interpersonal interaction.

Cognition

Figure 5 shows that a decision maker responds to a number of stimuli: personal needs, requirements of the job, interaction with others, and demands in the external environment. However, one also responds to internal pressures as well. How the individual reacts to these stimuli is considered "perception." That is, the way we take in information depends on our cognitive complexity. Thus, for example, a person with low cognitive complexity will filter out much of the information received. At this first stage, we experience "perceptual bias" because of past experience, self-image, values, or sense of security, all of which can influence what we are "willing" to see or to respond to.

To explore this model further, we will examine which factors in executives' decision making depend on the way they think about problems. Mental processing of information depends on the following:

1. Receptivity: recognizing when there is a need to make a decision.
2. Perception: taking in or sensing relevant data or information.
3. Cognition: mentally processing the data perceived and integrating them with prior knowledge, concepts, or understanding.
4. Volition: "choosing" what to do about what we have perceived and our understanding of that perception. Underlying this element are the fundamental beliefs and values that often act as filters or constraints in terms of what choices will be made.
5. Action: implementing the decision and determining the consequences or results that can be expected from the choice made.

These five elements form the foundation for the executive's thought processes. The "decision process," in turn, is the means whereby we deal with decision situations. There are, therefore, two aspects to consider in decision making. One relates to the manner in which our brain processes information and solves problems. The second is how we go about implementing the decision once it is made.

The research on brain hemispheric specialization helps us to understand one aspect of decision style. People either have a predilection to focus on tasks or technical dimensions, using the left hemisphere, or a predilection to focus on social concerns and to rely on the emotional or feeling function of the right hemisphere.

A second aspect is the level of complexity with which the mind is able to deal. Some people have a high tolerance for ambiguity and are able to sort and organize complex situations easily within their minds. Others are more literal and rely heavily on knowing exactly what is presented to them. These people generally require a great deal of structure in order to perform well. Cognitive complexity reveals a person's capacity to cope with information or, more precisely, with quantities of positive and negative stimuli. People who reveal a relatively low capacity to deal with the details emanating from a company's reports or financial information take any steps to buffer themselves from the information or channel it to someone else. This is typical of people with a comparatively low analytical style, especially if they are not aware of the effect their style is having on their ability to handle information. On the other hand, individuals who have a high tolerance for ambiguity are at home in complex situations that are ill defined and that deal with large amounts of information. These two dimensions—the way people acquire information and the complexity with which they can handle it (cognitive complexity), on the one hand, and the side of their brain with which they process it, on the other hand— are fundamental to our description of decision styles.

We use the left brain/right brain effects to understand certain aspects of cognition. For example, our more primitive brain functions tend to be primarily action or time oriented. This would correspond to the lower cognitively complex styles, whereas our cerebral cortex and associative memory functions would tend to correspond more closely with the cognitively complex styles. The left brain, being our logical hemisphere, focuses on the more technical aspects of the world we perceive, while the right brain concentrates on the spatial, visual, or social aspects of our environment.

The Decision Process

As with the cognitive process, the decision process (outlined in Figure 6) also has five elements. These are:

1. Stimulus: the pressure or need that acts as an input to the decision maker. In turn, the response depends on the context or situation in which the stimulus is received.
2. Decision making: the factors that determine how executives respond to the stimulus.

Figure 6. The Decision Process.

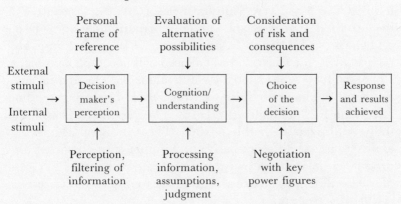

3. Problem solving: the way in which executives think about problems—whether they are dealt with in a direct and analytical manner or in a creative and intuitive manner.
4. Implementation: the carrying out of decisions. This element involves leadership, support, and understanding. How the decision maker interacts with others in the organization affects his or her ability to have decisions "accepted."
5. Results: in the final analysis, the results element determines the effectiveness of executives in managing their organizations and accomplishing goals.

While there may appear to be overlap between the cognitive process and the decision process, the latter is concerned with how our brain is used to process information, solve problems, make decisions, and take actions needed to achieve results. For example, in the decision process, factors such as politics, personal needs, and external pressures are all relevant. Another important consideration is the way in which we take in information. Perceptual bias or filtering of information is concerned with what is termed our attitude structure (Schroder, Driver, and Streufert, 1967). An individual's attitude structure may be absolute or rigid, or, at the other extreme, it may be very flexible. The rigid attitude has been used to describe the authoritarian, dogmatic individual whose belief becomes the basis for

defining one's "self." Perceptual bias, then, can be considered
the result of a concrete attitude structure that is insensitive to
the situation or to new and subtle information changes. Decision makers who "react" to situations are often dogmatic and
typically become frustrated when faced with a complex problem.
Rokeach (1960) considered these individuals as "closed minded,"
reluctant to change opinions on the basis of data but tending
to rely on instinct or fixed precepts. At the other extreme are
individuals who are highly flexible. These individuals have the
ability to relate different perceptual inputs to one another and
produce a meaningful picture. They tend to have a high level
of self-confidence and are able to relate to others and to resolve
conflicting perceptions.

Alignment

How each individual confronts the external world and
responds to the four forces is determined by his or her cognitive
complexity and environmental propensity. We consider an individual in "alignment," or in a state of equilibrium, when
cognitive complexity and environmental propensity are appropriately related to the demands imposed by the four primary
forces. When there is alignment (Culbert and McDonough,
1980) between an individual's style and the environmental requirements of a specific job, task, or career, the individual
derives satisfaction from his or her work. In turn, this satisfaction leads to:

1. Positive reinforcement. This results from satisfaction in productive behavior, as described by Skinner (1965). In turn,
   it has a positive influence on work performance.
2. Intrinsic rewards. These are related to the individual's level
   of satisfaction.
3. Higher motivation. The result is a positive commitment
   toward work performed.

The metaphor of amplification helps to explain the notion of
alignment. When two electrical waves "coincide" in frequency,
the amplitude of the incoming signal will be increased and thus

"amplify" the energy available. Similarly, "alignment" leads to increased satisfaction and positive reinforcement, which in turn contributes to improved performance through greater psychic energy. The opposite effect can also be predicted: Lack of alignment tends to lead to negative reinforcement and decreased performance. This "negalignment" inhibits commitment to the organization or willingness to compromise on decisions and ultimately can lead to frustration, avoidance, and withdrawal.

As can be seen, alignment, or the lack of it, is a key element in managerial effectiveness and executive success. How often have we heard about the proverbial square peg being forced into a round hole? This lack of alignment occurs because of our inability to correctly measure style and in turn to determine the behavioral variables that are required for effective performance of a given job. Recognizing that alignment is important, what can be done to correct a situation in which there is misalignment? The following are a number of potential interventional approaches that can be used to improve alignment: (1) a change in organization structure and/or realignment of authority of responsibility; (2) effective selection of individuals on the basis of both qualifications and style; (3) improved counseling and/or training regarding career selection and career paths; and (4) consideration of style as a means to evaluate relationships between the individual and peers and/or superiors. Decision styles can be used to predict how a person will react to a given decision situation. For example, Peter Oster, whom we discussed in Chapter One, was an individual with a high conceptual style that fit the requirements of some tasks but was out of alignment with the requirements to deal with group demands, personal needs, and environmental pressures.

The human mind is indeed a paradox. Perception is extraordinarily complex and is, in many respects, the basis of problem solving. The manager who does not respond appropriately to stimuli, who does not perceive problems, who does not instinctively and intuitively know how to respond, who cannot handle the analytical techniques required, and who has personality traits that either prevent or interfere with the process cannot cope effectively with decision making.

Decision Choices

The last stage of the process is concerned with choices we make and our willingness to follow through on decisions. This stage is related to satisfaction with work performed. Where there is alignment between a decision style and demands of the environment, there is a greater likelihood that we will choose actions that will reinforce the decisions we make. At this stage, interacting with peers, meeting personal needs, and responding to past environmental demands become significant aspects of the choices that are made.

We can see from the above discussion that the decision process ties together our ability to perceive information, to process that information, and to choose what we will do about our understanding of the information. Style defines our ability to perceive and process information, while the Four Force Model relates to the choices that we make regarding that information. In this sense, the combination of style and four force approach helps to clearly identify key elements of decision making, problem solving, performance, interpersonal competence, and environmental awareness.

Our examination of the decision process was intended to illustrate the relevance of information sensing (perception) and information usage (cognition) to the decisions that are made in organizations. Decision style, then, is the mirror that reflects an individual's personality. When combined with the individual's environmental concerns, a fairly complete picture of decision making emerges.

Change in Decision Styles

While individuals are able to adapt to changing job requirements, they seldom change their fundamental decision styles. The ability to change depends on (1) which decision style is dominant, (2) the level of stress, (3) the age or maturity of the individual, and (4) environmental conditions. The ability to change style was discussed in Rokeach's (1960) research, which suggests that a rigid person has difficulty in adapting to new conditions. Thus, a predominately directive individual might tend to favor a rule-abiding pattern rather than innovating new solutions. In contrast, an individual with a high tolerance for ambiguity might tend to be more adaptive. On the basis of our definitions for each style, reaction to stress, motivation, and perception can be described as shown in Table 3.

Table 3. Managerial Style Reactions.

Styles	Under Stress	Is Motivated by	Reacts to Stimuli by Using	Stimuli Are Seen as
Directive	Becomes annoyed	Power/status	Intuition	Linear
Analytical	Follows rules	Challenge	Insight	Logical
Conceptual	Searches Erratically	Recognition	Judgment	Relational
Behavioral	Avoids the Situation	Acceptance	Instinct	Emotional

A number of studies have been conducted on the effect of stress and information overload on decision styles. Research by Schroder, Driver, and Streufert (1967) indicated that all styles change the amount of information usage as load increases. Rowe, Mason, and Dickel (1985) indicated that decision style shifts as a function of stress. Hersey and Blanchard (1972) suggest that decision style changes with the age or maturity of an individual. This conclusion is supported by the research of Greiner (1973), who showed that older managers were "more considerate" than younger managers. Studies by Rowe and Boulgarides (1983) show that students' scores in the directive and behavioral style categories tend to differ from those of older individuals. Younger people have lower directive scores but higher behavioral scores than do older managers. This may be attributed to a younger person's lack of self-confidence or experience.

Three examples that illustrate the effect of stress on decision style are presented in Table 4. An examination of Table 4 reveals that all three individuals shifted to a more highly directive style when under stress. The pressure on the professor was related to time demands, whereas the company president and vice-president were under pressure because of poor sales and the possibility that the company might declare bankruptcy. Although the professor shifted from a highly conceptual style to a directive style, his score for the directive was above average prior to the stress situation. This illustrates that a backup style can readily be assumed

Table 4. Effect of Stress on Decision Style.

	Professor of Business		Company President		Company Vice-President	
	Normal	Stress	Normal	Stress	Normal	Stress
Directive	83	104	72	99	83	92
Analytical	64	62	91	68	108	89
Conceptual	103	89	65	57	59	69
Behavioral	50	45	67	76	50	50

when needed. The president and vice-president both had backup analytical scores prior to the onset of pressure, and, as expected, the shift in these cases was to a directive style.

In examining changes in style, Janis and Mann (1977) have reviewed several studies that indicate that people resist changing their habitual problem-solving approaches and are inclined to ignore suggestions about improving decision-making procedures. Janis and Mann concluded that ''People will show strong resistance to any intervention designed to change their approach to the tasks of search and appraisal when making an important decision unless all the conditions are present that foster vigilance. When the decision maker's dominant pattern is defensive avoidance, efforts made by a counselor to improve the quality of search and appraisal procedures are likely to be ignored or subverted unless he can increase the client's hope of finding a solution that will be better than that of the objectionable ones being contemplated. Unconflicted adherence, unconflicted change, and hypervigilance require different types of interventions to change the underlying psychological conditions in a way that will foster vigilance'' (p. 372).

Summary

The following summary helps to provide an overall perspective of the DSI and its underlying theories:

1. All individuals find themselves embedded in an environment that we call their decision situation.
2. The external conditions place demands on the individual.
3. These demands can be classified into four categories: per-

sonal needs, task requirements, social group demands, and environmental pressures.

4. All individuals tend to have a consistent internal psychological state.

5. This state can be adequately described in terms of whether the person is high or low in cognitive complexity and whether the person is oriented toward objective/task or subjective/people aspects in the external world. This we call environmental propensity. The combination of these factors results in four basic styles.

6. The DSI, using the concepts above and the responses to its twenty questions, helps to classify people's styles in a way that relates back to the four forces.

7. By use of the scores of the many people who have taken the DSI, a norm has been determined that shows where any individual fits in relation to the population as a whole. This is used for classifying one's style.

8. The individual should be able to evaluate his or her decision situation and determine the degree of alignment on the basis of style and the four forces.

9. The role of management is to achieve maximum alignment for each individual and for the organization as a whole. This is achieved by means of:

   a. Changing the individual's external conditions; for example, job design.

   b. Moving the individual to new external conditions; for example, making a career change.

   c. Changing the individual's style (this is very difficult except under conditions of stress).

   d. Having the individual accommodate to the given conditions. This is possible only if the person is adequately effective in using a less preferred style and/or is compensated for working with a less preferred style.

Now that you have tried the DSI, and with this theory in hand, we will turn to the question of how to use decision styles to manage more effectively. A more complete description of the underlying theories that support the developments described here will be presented in Chapters Nine and Ten.

5

●11●11●11●11●11●11●11●11●11●11●11●11●11●11●11●11●11●11●11●11●11●11●11●11●11●11●11●11●

Working with Different Styles:
How to Effectively
Interact with People
and the Organization

One cold and murky February afternoon, Jim Paisley was told
that he no longer was president of his company. The company
converted composite high-technology materials for use in home
construction, and Paisley had recently acquired a patent for the
technique. But the company had been bought out, and he
learned that there was no place for him in the new organization. "It was devastating," said Paisley. "How do you go home
and tell the wife that everything that you had built was suddenly
going in a different direction?" The same afternoon that he was
told that he was no longer needed in the new company, Paisley
called the cadre of handpicked employees that he had pulled
together four years previously. He told them, "I am very sorry
but we've been bought out by a larger fish who doesn't need
any of our services." With that, he trudged home to break the
news to his wife (Okun, 1987, p. 12).

    Why was there no place for Paisley in the new organiza-
tion? The new directors apparently wanted a caretaker, not an
innovator. They wanted to focus on generating cash, which requires a highly directive style, whereas Paisley's was an ana-
lytical/conceptual style. The new management concluded that
he did not fit their requirements. Is this an unusual case? Not

really. In case after case of an acquisition, we see the new management install a new team that fits their objectives.

As any experienced manager knows, managing an organization requires more than personality or energy or intelligence. Managers interact with individuals both inside and outside of the organization. They sometimes make decisions that go against the grain of the advice of staff, and they have the vision to see opportunity and potential where none existed before. How can we apply what we know about style to determine how executives manage their organizations?

Style can be used in any organization to discover the patterns that emerge in order to understand differences that exist in people. Of what value is this knowledge? By understanding their own styles and the styles of others, managers are in a better position to understand organizations and their managerial needs and to design organizations that can effectively relate to external conditions.

Most of our lives, we do the things that come naturally without reflecting very much on them. Sometimes these habits work for us, and sometimes they do not. We seldom know why. The language of style helps us to understand the reasons for these successes and failures and provides some clues as to how and what to change. If we understand style, we are better able to deal with others in the organization. We can help align individuals with positions that best suit their styles. The following case is an example of how alignment evolves over a long period of time and often with many traumatic incidents that include disalignment, frustration, erratic behavior, and, finally, realignment.

A Case Study

Jerry Westman grew up in New York and graduated in the top one-third of his class from Rensselaer Polytechnic Institute. Although his father was a mechanical engineer, Westman preferred electronics and mathematics and concentrated in those fields in his studies. Upon graduation, he accepted a job with a semiconductor firm near San Jose, California, where he and his new bride moved. At his new job, he was assigned to work for a lead engineer, who put him to work on a project involving the design of a computer program that could model the layout of memory chips. It was an exciting and challenging job for Westman. He soon became totally absorbed in his work, but he did manage to save a little time for his favorite hobby— writing cryptographic routines on his personal computer.

Westman soon became an expert on "read only memories" (ROMs) and made valuable contributions to the design of the company's ROM chip. These early successes led to various assignments that drew heavily on his technical expertise. In short succession, he became the de facto designer of an "erasable programmable read only memory chip" (EPROM) and an "electrically alterable read only memory chip" and then developed a computer-aided system that greatly speeded up the design of this class of chips. Throughout this period, Westman had a bubbly personality. Although he was a loner and shy, he was friendly, smiling, and easy to get along with. He was often heard to say, "This job is so much fun, it is a wonder I get paid to do it." Everybody liked him, as well as respecting his talent. Then he was promoted to a managerial position.

When Westman was made director of new product planning, he was ecstatic. He and his wife broke out the champagne, hired a babysitter—they had a daughter now—and drove to San Francisco, where they checked into the Fairmont Hotel for the weekend. They ate at Ernie's, listened to jazz at the Blue Note, and generally celebrated the promotion. Westman was happy not just with the increased salary but also with the opportunity to see some of his ideas infused into the company's strategy.

Despite his initial successes, he felt that the company executives had been recalcitrant about accepting many of his suggestions. He thought that in his new job he would be in a position to have a more direct impact on the company's direction. The first morning on the job, Westman arrived at about 7:30 and began to unpack his briefcase and organize things on his desk. Ten minutes later, one of his subordinates stuck his head in the door and asked whether he could come in. He announced that he was leaving to become part of a new start-up company in Silicon Valley. What bothered Westman most about the subordinate's decision was that he was the lead developer of a product that the company had hoped to announce within a few months. Westman worried that he would take the company's ideas with him to the new company.

Soon after the subordinate left Westman's office, John Richardson, the vice-president of manufacturing, called to set up a meeting with Westman later in the day. The precise reason for the meeting was not stated, but the message was clear. There were problems in the planning for the efficient manufacturing and quality control of products in the field. He wanted to be sure that Westman was fully aware of these problems and see to it that "manufacturing and quality control didn't have to carry so much of the burden in the future." Then Westman's secretary arrived. After a few pleasantries, she complained that she had been promised a new word processor several months ago. Would he look into it and see what he could do?

These incidents replayed themselves many times during the next few months, with new players and different themes and in a variety of surroundings but with a consistent effect. Westman was spending almost all of his time with people, all of whom placed demands on him. He had no time to design new products. In fact, no one seemed to want him to do that. Instead, he was involved in hundreds of decisions concerning organizational and personnel policies of the company. He was not very attentive to these decisions—he considered them a bother and a distraction—and as a consequence, many of them were made poorly.

As it became clear that Westman's office was not running smoothly and that many of the activities that he was involved in were in trouble, senior management became disenchanted with his performance. The meetings that he ran were disasters. He did not listen well—his mind was on his design ideas—and he lacked sensitivity to other people's feelings and needs. His reaction to this was to try to involve more people and to have more meetings. He became angry in most of these sessions, because the people seemed so slow and were taking up so much of his time. People's reactions in turn were to get as far away from him as they could. Finally, he realized that he was not doing well and that he definitely was not happy in his job. He became frustrated and then depressed. He tried the typical Silicon Valley remedies—a new computer, a new Ferrari, drinking, carousing—with the predictable results—economic difficulties, a strained marriage, problems on the job, and deep inner unhappiness. Meanwhile, his company was losing market share in ROM chips to a couple of domestic and Japanese companies.

Westman's DSI scores were analytical 102, directive 77, conceptual 73, and behavioral 48—a typical "engineer's" left brain style. The high analytical score explained why he was so well aligned with the design job. In this work, he could involve himself totally in analysis and research. There was always an objective solution to the design problems he dealt with. His mind need only traverse countless permutations of the "and" and "or" gates that could be integrated into a tiny piece of silicon. And this he did well, because his style, analytical coupled with directive, meant that he was very much a thinking, factual, objective kind of person. His difficulties arose when his managerial job forced him into intense one-on-one interpersonal sessions and many group meetings. His low behavioral and modest conceptual styles simply did not provide him with the feelings, the sensitivities, and the people orientation necessary to be effective in his new role. He further compounded his difficulties, as many people do, by lashing out with his behavioral shadow side, calling ill-fated meetings and engaging in hostile sessions with his colleagues.

For some time, Westman did not know what was happening to him, why he had been so effective and happy in one role and was so miserable in the other. After he took the DSI, he was able to understand the problem and to talk about it. Analytical design work fit his style perfectly, and that is why, when he was designing chips, he reached that high level of involvement that Larry Bird and Tim Gallwey do. In that involved state, he was among the best at what he did. The heavy interpersonal burden of a managerial job placed him in a position that was antithetical to his style. Worse yet, he did not understand that his low behavioral score accounted for part of the problem.

In situations of disalignment, people tend to do one of two things. Some, as Westman did, flail out and attempt to use a style that is uncomfortable to them. Because it is their inferior function and they are inexperienced in using it, they usually have poor results. As matters get worse, other people see them as inconsistent and "out of character." Others, like the defeated bulls in Hemingway's *Farewell to Arms* who retreat to the spot in the ring whence they will make their dying stand, withdraw into their dominant style, which is usually inappropriate for the task at hand. Westman did a little bit of this, too. He tried to solve through analysis and authority problems that really required compassion and understanding.

Obviously, decision style alone will not determine whether an individual will succeed in a job, but it does show which jobs an individual would find most satisfying. Westman was extremely happy as an engineer and received considerable positive reinforcement in the form of intrinsic rewards as well as pay increases and promotion. However, his new position as a manager not only deprived him of job satisfaction but actually contributed negative reinforcement because of his inability to cope with the kinds of problems that confronted him.

The answer is not to pigeonhole a person such as Westman in the role of an engineer. Rather, if both Westman and his management had known his style, they could have handled the promotion differently. For example, rather than making him director of new product planning, they could have given him greater responsibility for developing new products and supervising a number of senior engineers. If he made a smooth transition into this new position, he could later assume more responsibility. For example, it is unlikely a good manager would lose a key engineer to competition without making an attempt to dissuade him or her. Westman lacked both an understanding of human behavior and the experience to deal with complex, highly unstructured behavioral problems.

If Westman could not handle the position of director, he could perhaps work with an assistant who was better at interpersonal relations than he was. Often, managing highly technical organizations requires a combination of two people, one whose expertise is left brain, analytical/directive, and one who is more right brain, conceptual/behavioral. Hughes Aircraft Company for many years has found this a workable procedure and has avoided the pitfall of putting people like Westman into the wrong position.

Westman's story, in fact, turned out well. It was during his period of frustration and depression that he attended a seminar at his company in which the DSI was used. After the meeting, he told us much of the story recounted above. He suggested that his decision style was likely inappropriate for the managerial job that he held and that perhaps that was the cause of his unhappiness. We agreed. From there on, we simply talked about what it means to have a match between one's style and the job. We examined his responses to the questions, especially those he marked with 8s and 1s. The 8 recorded next to "Others consider me disciplined and precise" and the 1 next to "supportive and compassionate" brought a smile to his lips and a small tear to his eye. "That's what everyone has been trying to tell me, I guess," he said, and he began to recount how anxious he became when person after person came into his office and unloaded his or her personal problems on him. "I am just not good at dealing with intense emotions."

Following the session, Westman took several positive steps. He went to see a counselor to get some professional psychiatric advice. After a long talk with his company's management, he was transferred to a position doing design research, a position he enjoyed. After about a year, he left to accept a research and development position with another company. He began to read and think about people and their emotions and to try to experience them—including attending a sensitivity training session—because he wanted to face up to his "inferior function." Perhaps most importantly, he began to spend more time at home with his wife, talking to her about their life together and what she meant to him. When we last talked to Westman, he was "back in the flow," his mind totally immersed in analyzing a new design for another chip for his new company.

Understanding Others' Styles

As the morning sun irradiated the whitecaps, the executive of an office equipment manufacturing firm found the drive along the ocean from Los Angeles to Santa Barbara was most enjoyable. His enjoyment was tempered somewhat, however, by a need to think through how to apply the Decision Style Inventory to the problem he was facing. He had posed a challenging question: Could the DSI be used to prepare market research analysts for customer reactions during interviews?

The problem arose in the context of recommending an interview schedule that had been the result of a corporate strategic planning exercise. The purpose of the interview was twofold. First, it was to obtain customers' evaluations of the performance of existing computer-based printing and reproduction equipment. Second, it was to obtain estimates of the future requirements for printing documents in the customers' organizations. A questionnaire had been prepared that would be administered by a market researcher during a series of personal interviews.

The executive expressed concern regarding the market research department's use over the previous few years of statistical analysis for direct mail questionnaires, which were analyzed to determine information about the focus group. As a result of this practice, few of the market research team had any interviewing experience, and time pressures did not permit a full training program. Yet the executive felt that these interviewers needed to be aware that people have different psychological styles and thus would respond in different ways to questions posed during an interview. For example, a problem with a printer might be expressed in one way by one customer and quite differently by another customer with a different style. The astute interviewer would have to be able to sift through these stylistic differences and determine whether the equipment deficiency, though expressed differently, was, in fact, the same problem.

This executive had participated in planning sessions in which the DSI and other instruments had been used to assign planners to different working groups. He was aware of the variation in perspective that people with different decision styles bring to bear on a planning problem. He was also impressed with how much he had learned about the way people think as a result of these working sessions. With this background, his challenge was whether he could construct an exercise that would help the market researchers become more aware of people's styles. The purpose of the study was to determine the market researchers' ability to identify stylistic factors during their interviews. The drive to Santa Barbara provided time to think about how to approach this problem and to assess how such an exercise might work.

The market researchers' retreat was held in the Biltmore Hotel in Santa Barbara, where a plenary room and three smaller rooms were reserved. Our presentation, first on the agenda, started about nine o'clock. After a short discussion of psychological styles and interpersonal aspects of interviewing, we administered the DSI. The objective was to form four working groups, each comprising individuals who were primarily analytical, conceptual, behavioral, or directive. As we had expected, most of the twenty-three people who participated were analytical and/or directive. In fact, almost all were either "left brain" (analytical/directive) or "upper half" (analytical/conceptual). Given these results, a "Kentucky windage" method for assigning people to working groups was devised. The one person who scored high in the behavioral style was assigned to that group. Then the four other people who had the highest behavioral scores, regardless of their primary style, were also assigned to that group. The remaining eighteen market researchers were divided into three groups of six people each on the basis of their highest DSI scores. In order to make this work, one of the people from the analytical group—the one with the highest conceptual score—was assigned to the conceptual group. In this way, each market researcher was assigned to one of the four groups without knowing which decision style it represented.

The task assigned to the working groups was one developed by Ian and Donna Mitroff (Mitroff and Mitroff, 1980). Each group was given a set of Tinker Toys with the following instructions: Your group has free reign to take the company in a new direction. Determine the customers' needs by designing a product using the Tinker Toys. Develop a sales presentation, which will be given in the plenary session at 1:00. A few researchers balked at the assignment as being too vague. Some felt that it was irrelevant to the crucial task at hand and wanted to get right into discussing the interview schedule. Initially, some of the groups faltered. Soon, however, leaders emerged in each group, and they decided to get on with the exercise, albeit with a bit of skepticism. As every football coach knows, once the players take to the field, the coach loses control over the process and must wait until the end of the game to know the final outcome.

At 1:00, the groups were called together, and the reporting process began. The directive group reported first. The customer need they identified was related to the recent great expansion of international business and the increase in companies doing business abroad. They developed an automated currency converter that would take in money from one country and convert it to the currency of any other. Their Tinker Toy assembly was symmetrical and well defined and used most of the pieces in the set. Their presentation stressed the need for a practical and useful product that could be produced in a relatively short period of time. The group then produced a series of flip charts that gave rather detailed specifications for the product. At the conclusion, they presented several charts that showed the specific exchange rates between currencies, to four decimal places, that would be in the initial memory of the system. The group spokesperson closed with a rather spirited and aggressive "asking for the order."

The analytical group presented their product next. As they unveiled it—white sheets were used by each group to hide their Tinker Toy creations until the dramatic moment—the spokesperson described how the group had undertaken a careful and thorough study of customer needs. This analysis showed that communications were the most pressing problem facing customers today. Drawing on principles of physics, the group had designed a "Zap" telecommunications machine that operated as a local area network, with a satellite transmitter and receiver, and when speed was of the essence, a document dematerializer and rematerializer. The Tinker Toy structure was logically constructed and had moving parts that simulated the functioning of an actual machine. A few seemingly errant parts rested on its top. When asked to explain them, one of the members spoke up. "That's a carrier pigeon. It's our backup system. We ac-

tivate it when all else fails.'' The presentation itself implored
the customers to examine their communications thoroughly and
to study this product carefully. The sales presentation closed
with a statement that if the customer followed this advice, the
logic of the product and its advantages would be obvious.

The behavioral group had the most difficulty organizing.
There was a sigh of relief when they brought their veiled product to the front of the room and finally seemed ready for the
presentation. The decision style of the first two groups had been
revealed rather strongly in their presentations; if the behavioral
group's was not, it was feared that attention would be focused
on the first two. The spokesperson—the only true behavioral
in the group—started by recounting the difficulties that the group
had had in getting started on their assignment. She explained
that she was elected spokesperson after she pleaded with them
to get together and complete the exercise. Everybody in the
group seemed to be waiting for someone else to make a proposal. Finally, one of the members asked her, ''What product
would you like to see us make?'' The only thing that came to
her mind was the need to solve a personal problem of her own.
''Fine,'' the group replied, ''you can be our customer. We'll
interview you and produce a product to fit your needs.'' She
described how the most pressing problem that she faced as a
single parent was teaching a fifteen-and-a-half-year-old daughter
how to drive so that when she became sixteen she could get her
license. Mother-daughter conflicts seemed to explode when the
two of them were in the car together, especially when the daughter was at the wheel. The tensions and anxieties were almost
unbearable. The remaining members of the group pressed her
for a more complete description of the problem and then turned their attention to developing a solution.

The behavioral group unveiled a computerized home driving simulator as their Tinker Toy creation. The student driver
had merely to sit in front of a three-dimensional display and
turn on the computer. Voice, sound, visuals, and animation
coordinated by an intelligent computer program presented the
driver with situations to which to respond using a mock steering wheel, pedals, and dashboard. The computer kept track of

each situation the driver faced and how it was handled. This information could then be used by the instructor to discuss in a calm environment any problems that the student faced. The sales presentation focused on an advertisement in which the announcer discussed the emotional problems that parents, especially single parents, have teaching their children to drive. It also described how difficult it was for the young driver as well. They closed by stating that compassionate parents would be able to reduce conflicts at home by purchasing their product.

The conceptual group was the last to make a presentation. They had been very secretive in their preparations and were completely silent as they set their hooded product on the table and each member quietly moved to his or her chair and sat down. After a short pause, the spokesperson arose and walked in a stately manner to the front. There was another pause. "Wouldn't you all like to feel better?" he asked in a soft basso voice. He waited until everybody nodded affirmatively. "Plants," he continued, "also like to feel good." He reached into his pocket and produced a handful of wooden coffee stirrers—the ones that look like Popsicle sticks. The bundle was passed around the room, and each of us was asked to take one stick for each plant we had in our house, up to a total of three sticks. Everybody took some sticks. Most took three. "That's our market research," he proclaimed. "You are all prospects for our new product."

Two members of the group came to the front and, one on either side of the white sheet, began to roll it up, revealing their creation. It was the simplest of machines. Using only a few of the Tinker Toy pieces, the group had constructed a small device. In the center, one of the round pieces functioned as a knob for tuning, and protruding from the top was a yellow trapezoidal piece. The spokesperson explained that the device was a soothing machine and would transmit comforting vibrations to plants in much the same way that fine music, soft lighting, and a calm ambience are beneficial for human growth. A woman then appeared from the wings. In each hand she held a plastic coffee cup. The cups were filled with soil, and there was a small piece of ivy in each, taken from the Biltmore's garden. Behind each of these tiny plants, a short Tinker Toy dowel was implanted. And in the slits of each dowel was a red trapezoidal piece. The woman explained that these were antennas. Periodically, the central unit would poll each plant and read its feeling meter. Whenever it encountered a plant that was not feeling well, it would review the symptoms and search its memory for the correct treatment. Then it would transmit a vibration signal, the cycles of which were calibrated to soothe the plant. The object of this was to create a state of harmony and serenity among all plants. The spokesperson and the woman with the plants speculated that once all the plants of the world were in harmony, perhaps we could achieve a world in which all of humanity was in harmony, too.

After the coffee break, the debriefing session was begun. First, the dominant decision style in each group was revealed, along with a discussion of the key characteristics of each style. Then the discussion turned to a critique of each group's presentation and how it revealed the group's dominant style. It was noted that the directive group presented by far the most specific facts of any group, that it was far more technical than the others, and that its sales presentation was the most aggressive. The analytical group also had a technical orientation, as would be expected; however, their design was based more on theory and analysis, and their sales approach appealed more than any other presentation to the customer's rationality and sense of logic. Both the behavioral and the conceptual groups' presentations were more people oriented. The behavioral group focused on people's needs, indeed the plight of a single parent, and from that developed a product and a sales approach that satisfied those needs. This individualized solution was then related to others that might have the same problem.

In contrast, the conceptual group's orientation was to people—or, more precisely, to living things in general. While the sales appeals of both of these groups were to the emotions and feelings of the potential customers, the behavioral group, drawing on its need to be specific, focused on the feelings of a single individual, whereas the conceptual group related to the feelings of humanity as a whole. The consensus was that the conceptual group's presentation was also the most original.

Overall, the people agreed that each group exhibited a different style and that this style was explainable by the DSI. To several members' surprise, the exercise had helped them to understand not only their own decision styles but those of others as well.

But what did this have to do with conducting interviews with customers regarding printers and paper? This question was dealt with on the second day of the retreat, devoted to reviewing the interview schedule. First, the reason for each question's being on the schedule was reviewed. Then, the information that the company wanted from the customer and why it was important to corporate planning were examined. Next, the questions were looked at from the respondent's point of view. Was there anything sensitive? Would the respondent really know the answer? Were there circumstances under which the respondent would not reveal the true answer to the interviewer? Finally, there was the question of style. The group was asked to speculate about how people with each style would answer the questions. Would they be able to conceptualize a customer's style, and on which aspects of the style would they focus?

This last inquiry proved to be quite interesting. Although the market researchers had limited experience with the company and little if any field experience, all of them were familiar with the company's equipment, its areas of competence, its shortcomings, and the kinds of complaints that customers made. The questions about equipment performance were the ones that generated the most lively discussion on style. One question in particular focused on a performance problem that the company had experienced with a printer and only recently had identified. Field representatives were at a loss as to how to diagnose the problem because the customers' reports were so varied. It was thought, therefore, that in the interviews, this question might generate many different responses.

The groups speculated on how people with each decision style would report the problem. This helped them to see that the same "real" technical problem might be filtered through the observer's decision style and thus be reported in different ways. These speculations were compared to previously received complaints—for which, in many cases, the underlying cause was not known, but which nonetheless had been recorded in the service logs and classified by the market researchers. Now, on thinking about it, the group felt that customers with a directive style were likely responsible for the complaints dealing with specific data regarding performance and demanding immediate repairs. Many of these complaints were a result of frustration because the customers lacked control over their operations. The customers with a behavioral style were the ones most likely to have responded to problems by personalizing them, often referring to them as personal tragedies. These complaints usually did not deal directly with the technical performance of the hardware itself but rather centered on the symptoms of poor performance as experienced by the customer or other individuals—often identified by name—who were affected by the problem. "This whole thing's a mess! Everybody is suffering! The entire company is affected!" This type of complaint likely came from the conceptual style. Finally, the analytical style was the likely source of complaints in which a problem was formulated and a possible solution was offered. Some of these complaints contained a rather complete analysis of the performance of the equipment. At the end of the day, every question on the interview schedule had been discussed in this way. The members of the group and the executive agreed that they now were better prepared to look for clues revealing the interviewee's style and to interpret his or her responses accordingly.

While this kind of experience lacks the rigor that researchers might prefer, the interviews were conducted successfully, and the company was pleased with the results and the quality of the data. Although the DSI was not administered to the customer interviewees, several of the interviewers reported that their awareness of style helped them in the interviews. Perhaps the best assessment came from the executive himself, who said, "I believe that the retreat was exactly what I wanted. It made the otherwise arduous task of working through a questionnaire lively and interesting. The awareness of decision style and a way to talk about it made the difference." This experience helps to illustrate how the concept of style can be used to explain people's behavior. The language of style gives us a way to understand others, especially when they are different from us. Several of the participants in the market research retreat were surprised when they discovered that other people's behavior was systematically different from their own, both in the Tinker Toy exercise and in the ways that customers complained about equipment.

Understanding another's style can be valuable in forming relationships. If you are working with a partner who is analytical, for example, it would be helpful to be aware that that person's focus will be on the technical aspects of a task and use of logic in thinking about possibilities. Analyticals are very cerebral, while a behavioral partner demands much more personal attention. Behaviorals prefer to share feelings directly without much intellectualizing. They listen, participate, and express concern for the well-being of their friends and colleagues. A directive, on the other hand, will approach a relationship in a much more impersonal way. He or she prefers order, status, power, and control in a relationship and will often be the initiator of activities in the relationship. A conceptual partner tends to express his or her feelings about the relationship as a whole and to view it from a longer time perspective. Details are not important, except perhaps as they are related to some broader concern. For example, a conceptual is likely to tolerate an unpleasant condition for a long time and then blow up over a minor detail, such as how the bed is made in the morning. This quickly escalates into a broad and abstract complaint of unhappiness. Neither the directive nor the behavioral acts that way. Their need for structure and concreteness expresses itself in a concern about specific events in a relationship. The behavioral complains that some event hurt his or her feelings and resulted in a sense of rejection, whereas the directive complains that an event caused anxiety and a sense of lost control. The analytical and, to some extent, the conceptual will complain about events that are mundane and boring. The conceptual is opposed to events in a relationship that restrict his or her freedom. The analytical is opposed to the routine events in a relationship that lack intellectual challenge or that conflict with his or her sense of logic.

How one style relates to another can be viewed from two perspectives: a person-to-person relationship or a manager's relationship to a group. The question is: what can style tell us about relationships between individuals? Is it better to have similar styles to achieve compatibility, or do opposites attract? The answer depends on the context and content of the relationship. There is little question that people with similar styles understand one another more easily than they understand someone with a different style. This is especially true in individuals with high cognitive complexity (analytical and conceptual), who cannot readily communicate with persons who prefer structure and who reject complexity. Conversely, the less complex individual (directive and behavioral) has a very low tolerance for the painstaking detail and length of explanation used by individuals with high cognitive complexity. The action-oriented individual has little tolerance for the thinker, whereas the thinker tends to be inept in action-oriented tasks and generally is uninterested in relationships that require action.

We can see that style helps explain relationships. We see this most clearly in strong leaders who look for similar attributes in subordinates. Fortunately, our research reveals that most executives have a high conceptual score and can tolerate most other styles because of their compassion and their ability to tolerate ambiguity. The highly directive, on the other hand, tends not to tolerate others who are different, because of both a low tolerance for ambiguity and a dominant need to control. They are compatible with "loyal" directive subordinates but tend to reject those who confront them or do not agree with their ideas. People with the analytical style, because of high cognitive complexity, relate best to other analyticals or to conceptuals who have an analytical bent. They do not understand the behavioral and find that the directive is not as careful or complete in what he or she does as the analytical would desire. In many organizations, analyticals will cluster with other analyticals and feel uncomfortable interacting with people with any other style. Witness, for example, how professionals such as engineers, accountants, and lawyers behave in social settings: they tend to talk with one another rather than mixing with others. Behaviorals, because of their need for affiliation, will generally try to please others. They are uncomfortable with directives, who tend to be authoritarian, and they rarely understand the analytical. They

Table 5. Compatibility Among Styles.

Subordinate:	Directive	Analytical	Conceptual	Behavioral
Leader:				
Directive	C	M	X	S
Analytical	M	C	M	X
Conceptual	X	M	C	C
Behavioral	S	X	C	C

Note: C = compatible; M = moderately compatible; S = slightly compatible; X = generally incompatible.

are generally most comfortable with either other behaviorals or conceptuals. In order to summarize these relationships, we have shown them in Table 5.

What we learn from the relationships shown in Table 5 is that people feel most comfortable with those who have similar styles. They do not always understand other styles and sometimes will alienate others. The language of style can facilitate an understanding of differences and whether one can readily accommodate to the differences. The following guidelines can be used when considering new assignments or restructuring organizational relationships.

Analyticals and conceptuals (upper half) need directives or behaviorals as partners to:

• provide realism to a situation
• bring up pertinent facts
• keep track of details
• check records, catalogue information
• remember things from the past, including people's names
• perform inspections and other action-oriented tasks
• attend to things that need to be done
• carry out orders
• have patience and be supportive

Directives and behaviorals (lower half) need analyticals or conceptuals as partners to:

• see new possibilities
• apply creativity or analysis to a problem

- deal with complexity and ambiguity
- explain analytical ideas or analysis
- look into the future and do broad planning

Analyticals and directives (left brain) need conceptuals or behaviorals as partners to:

- deal with people and social problems, especially with others' feelings
- persuade or convince people
- visualize material and teach others
- stimulate and arouse enthusiasm
- conciliate or compromise when needed

Conceptuals and behaviorals (right brain) need analyticals and directives as partners to:

- get things done
- carry out reforms
- focus on problems and do appropriate analysis
- organize data and establish controls
- predict and find potential flaws
- carefully weigh evidence and facts
- maintain consistency in policies
- stand firm against opposition

The following are guidelines for finding a partner for a manager with a given decision style:

1. *Directive.* Match with a conceptual or behavioral who is a catalyst type and who will emphasize people and humanistic issues while the directive provides direction and structure to the undertaking and keeps it running efficiently.
2. *Behavioral.* Match with an analytical who can furnish new technology and analysis of ideas. This type often needs a "clean-up" person to provide order to his or her life, doing such things as writing reports, accumulating data, recording decisions and ideas as they are made, undertaking

unpleasant jobs, and providing reminders. Match with a directive to get some "tough decisions" made, especially those that might hurt people's feelings.

3. *Analytical*. Match with a directive to serve as a troubleshooter and fact finder. Or match with a conceptual to generate ideas for analysis and to explain the analytical and his or her work to others. This type often must be provided with "go-fors" who will carry out details. Match with behavioral when sensitive people-oriented issues are important or there are concerns about psychological stress, the physical environment, health, or comfort.

4. *Conceptual*. Match with a directive to provide stability, administer and implement rules and regulations, and carry out policies. These people need a "go-for" and a detail person. An analytical will help them determine the implications of their needs and to "flesh" them out.

Style also helps us to understand the contradictions that we sometimes observe in people. Whenever someone performs differently from what we expect, it may be that his or her shadow style is being used. That was the case with Peter Oster, who was described in Chapter One. When he was placed in a job that did not match his style and he was under stress, Oster's behavior became dysfunctional. People under stress often retreat into the directive style for short periods, whether it is their preferred style or not. The shift to a directive style under stress is understandable. Information cannot be processed because of the emotional overload, and it is difficult to think clearly because of the interference caused by the stressful situation. Lack of time also prevents careful thinking when there is pressure to complete a task in a short period. We can summarize typical behaviors for each style when under stress thus: the directive becomes angry or explodes and yells; the analytical shifts to a focused, directive style; the conceptual becomes erratic in searching for an appropriate response; and the behavioral tends to avoid the situation and withdraws. The directive's quest for immediate action is functional when it is a natural style. However, when it is an unnatural style, imposed by external events, it often takes the form of lashing out to make decisions and to reduce anxiety at all costs. Sometimes the response is bizarre. The language of style cautions us to ask whether this unusual behavior is due to an underdeveloped style being forced on the individual.

Conclusion

Managing with style emphasizes the interactions that take place in organizations. As we will see in the next chapter, style is not the sole determinant of effective management. We must consider the organizational environment—its culture, norms, values, and sentiments—to have a more complete picture of what relations occur in an organizational setting. Nonetheless, relationships do exist, and there are interactions that are dependent on the styles of the individuals involved. If we understand those relationships, we are in a better position to have a smoothly running organization and less conflict. For example, the highly directive president of Eagle Manufacturing discovered late one afternoon that a critical proposal to a major customer that had to be delivered that evening had not been completed. Exasperated, he called in his secretary to find out what had happened. To his annoyance, she told him that she was leaving to cook dinner for her in-laws. Barely able to restrain himself, he bellowed, "Don't you know how important that proposal is!" Cringing, she replied, "I'm terribly sorry, but I refuse to anger my in-laws after meeting them only once." In a bellicose voice, the president countered, "Don't bother to come back Monday. We'll mail you your check!"

Who was right? The president, whose only concern was to get out the proposal, or the secretary, who was concerned about alienating her in-laws? In one sense, neither was right. Firing the secretary certainly did not get the proposal done on time; on the other hand, the secretary showed a disregard for meeting a critical deadline. If the president had been more analytical, he would have realized that, rather than the secretary cooking a meal, he could send out to the fanciest caterer in town to bring in the meal and let the secretary finish the typing. Unfortunately, this was not his style, and he lost not only the contract but a competent employee as well.

How often do we observe what would appear to be irrational behavior only to learn that we could readily explain it by the language of style? Would this help us to change a person's behavior? Probably not. The president of Eagle would not countenance an employee who was not absolutely loyal to the organization over all other matters. He would not change. Then what does the language of style offer? For those individuals who are reasonably flexible, it provides an awareness of what is going on and possible ways of handling difficult situations.

Training has proved useful as a means for better understanding why decisions are made in the way that they are. We saw this in the example of learning how to interpret customer complaints. Because style provides a valuable perspective concerning people's behavior, it offers the astute executive a means for gaining insights that might otherwise prove elusive and difficult to come by. It is a powerful tool for those that choose to use it, and it can contribute to greater effectiveness in a managerial role.

6

●II●II●II●II●II●II●II●II●II●II●II●II●II●II●II●II●II●II●II●II●II●II●II●II●II●II●II●II●II●II●

Understanding How
Style Works in the Organization

Many organizations evolve, as Emerson said, as "the lengthened shadow of one man." They reflect the leader's flair, pace, and deepest values. The executive's leadership shapes them so that the organization and the executive become, as it was said of Geneen and ITT, "inseparable." The organizational style and management style become one.

IBM under Thomas Watson, Sr., was an example of an organization with a directive leader. It was a highly structured organization with a smart dress code that stressed attention to detail and practical results. There was a strong hierarchy in the structure, and every CEO since Watson has sought to be in control, though none so vigorously as the founder. Ken Olson at Digital Equipment Corporation (DEC) runs a more conceptual organization. It is based on ideas, new approaches, and an aura of personal freedom. Hewlett-Packard reflects the more behavioral tendencies of Bill Hewlett and David Packard. Flextime, job sharing, quality control circles, and other participative methods have flourished at Hewlett-Packard, and the corporate policy is concerned with individuals and their personal needs. Seymore Cray and Gene Amdahl created organizations in their own analytical images. Our experience with people such as these suggests that Cray Research and Amdahl Corporation and Trilogy Limited are companies that stress problem solving and logical analysis. Their people look for intellectual challenges and expect the logic of their products to persuade customers to buy

90

them. A leader's style permeates an organization for both good and bad. Each of the above-mentioned organizations has been successful, in part, because it has been a reflection of the leader's effective use of his style. But as Kets de Vries and Miller (1984) have described in their comprehensive study on *The Neurotic Organization,* the neuroses and psychopathologies of leaders often infuse their organizations and lead them astray. In addition, times change, and the style that was appropriate for one era or set of environmental conditions may be grossly inappropriate for another. What happens, then, when an executive's style no longer fits the needs of the organization?

Increasingly, corporations have had to ask themselves this question. The language of style is one of the tools that they can use for answering that very difficult question. The board of directors at ITT, for example, had to ask themselves this question late in 1973, when corporate performance began to wane. Technological and political changes were placing new demands on the company's growing and complex international telecommunications business. The hard-driving directive style of Harold Geneen was no longer appropriate. Geneen himself seemed to sense this need for change. In a *Business Week* article ("Harold Geneen's Tribulations," 1973), he commented on policy problems in Chile and spoke of ITT's central role in the economy there. He spoke to the needs of underdeveloped countries and called for participatory management in corporate and public affairs throughout the world, exactly what the board had found lacking in his leadership during those last few years. It was as if he were setting out an agenda for his successor. Within a few weeks after Geneen left, a new CEO, Tom Dunleavy, was appointed. His style was quite different from Geneen's. He was also tough, but he was more conceptual, and so better able to deal with the massive intellectual problem of understanding and guiding a worldwide telecommunications industry; more statesmanlike, and so better able to deal with politics in many different countries; and more behavioral, and so better able to deal with the substantial personnel problems that were festering within the company. In short, the board believed that Dunleavy had the style and the talent that ITT's new situation called for.

Style can be useful in the design of organizations. An organization's very success depends on its ability to coordinate the contributions of people with diverse backgrounds. Organizations and communities that are well designed provide meaningful relationships. They include people from all walks of life, from the assembly line worker to the scientist and even the artist. Thus, they have within their repertoire of resources a broad range of backgrounds and experience. Just as every individual has some capacity in each of the four styles, so too do viable organizations. Organizations are collections of people with different styles, ideally with each one assigned to a role that fits his or her style.

The Honda Case. Consider the history of the Honda Motor Company. Sochiro Honda was considered the world's number one founding president. He was a fiery individual, bubbling with ideas and excitement. Like Edwin Land, he was an inventive genius who was deeply involved in working on his product. He had a conceptual style with a strong behavioral backup. The legend goes that as a young child he was enthralled by the first automobile he saw. He stroked his hand across the motor, felt the oil, rubbed it into his hands, sniffed and savored it, and dreamed that one day he would be building his own motorcar. From that day on, he spent long and intensive hours contemplating engines and cars and experimenting with them. An intense desire rose within him to build racing motorcycles, to race them himself, and to win. He formed a business to carry out his dream and to support him in achieving his most cherished ambition: to win the world-renowned international race at the Isle of Man.

When he was not racing, Honda was involved with his company. He was very close to his employees and spent almost all his time with them on the shop floor. He addressed everybody by first name and would move—some called it "skip"—from bench to bench discussing problems and providing encouraging pep talks. The motorcycle was his love. He was given more to flair than to the details of production and business. In fact, his business practices were rather flamboyant. He once stripped naked on a bench top in order to demonstrate to his employees how to properly assemble his motorcycle. He was a partier and a bit of a philanderer. He was frequently seen—and heard—cruising through the streets of Tokyo on one of his new cycles. His cycle was often seen parked in front of a geisha house. In one reckless moment, he reportedly threw a geisha out of a second-story window. This careless attitude infused his business activities as well. At a crucial period in his company's history when he rather urgently needed financing, he prepared for a meeting with the staid and conservative Sumitomo Bank by drinking heavily and then, adorned in costume, appeared and delivered an impassioned, inebriated plea for funds. He was turned down. And the company was in trouble.

Honda and his supporters soon realized that he needed someone else in his organization to offset his flamboyant style. He found the right person in Takeo Fujisawa. In 1949, Honda and Fujisawa became partners. Fujisawa was a practicing financial analyst with a liking for accounting. His style was a combination of directive and analytical. While Honda dreamed of new and faster motors and of winning races in exotic places, Fujisawa worried about balance sheets, market shares, cash flow, and the myriad of mundane details necessary to run a business. Like Harold Geneen, Fujisawa was an ardent accumulator of specific facts. He would carefully sift through the mounds of data that he collected and look for clues for new directions for the company. He was looking for solid business opportunities as well as immediate practical results.

This diligence paid off early in the partnership. Fujisawa had assembled a set of data that covered the sales and usage patterns of motorcycles and other vehicles throughout Japan. These facts revealed an untapped potential market: Japanese housewives were currently using bicycles to run their domestic errands. He challenged Sochiro Honda's creative genius. Could Honda develop a small motorcycle for the Japanese housewife, one that was safe, inexpensive, and easy to drive on crowded city streets? Always up to a challenge, Honda threw himself into the project. The result was the Honda 50cc Supercub, a sort of motor scooter that revolutionized the motorcycle business.

In 1958, when it was announced, sales began to skyrocket, first in Japan, then throughout the world. Hondas were seen everywhere, and the Honda Motor Company was on its way to success. Fujisawa became Honda's alter ego. His directive and analytical tendencies counterbalanced Honda's conceptual genius. While he prodded Honda to innovate in areas where profitable markets existed, Honda, in turn, prodded him to keep the company financially solvent and organizationally strong. They became an effective partnership, a community of differences in style bound by a common objective.

If we understand decision style, we can find many examples of "marriages" such as Honda and Fujisawa's. Effective communities and partnerships are made of marriages in which the union is greater than the sum of the parts. Successful organizations continue to search for these unions, especially among their top management teams.

Lotus Development Corporation. The Lotus Development Corporation undertook a similar search for an effective partnership of styles. Mitchell D. Kapor, the company's founder, together with Jonathan Sachs, had conceived of and developed Lotus 1-2-3, an immensely popular spreadsheet software program that extended the VisiCalc computer program. Through very clever organization and programming, Kapor and Sachs were able to produce a spreadsheet program for a microcomputer that accommodated more rows and columns, was faster, and had more capabilities, especially graphics and data-base management capacity, than any other program available. Because of its menu structure, it was also easier to use than other programs. Lotus 1-2-3 was "user friendly," as the jargon goes. It was a startling success almost from the day in February 1983 when it was released. This very success, however, put great stress on Kapor and his organization. He was a theoretician who liked to think of new ideas and products. Running a high-volume business required attention to detail that he simply did not enjoy.

As sales grew, Kapor realized that he needed a more business-oriented person in the organization. In 1983, he offered the job of director of corporate marketing to James P.

Manzi, an analyst with McKinsey & Company who had prepared a business plan for Lotus. Manzi rose quickly in the firm. Within a year, he was made vice-president of sales and marketing; he became president in 1984. In 1986, he was appointed CEO in place of Kapor, who became the new president. While Kapor was clearly the theoretical and creative force behind the company, explained business analysts, Manzi was its nuts-and-bolts man, and the changes in job titles merely reflected differing interests and styles. It was natural that they would gravitate toward what each one did best.

The Astrotek Story. What happens when an organization is confronted with conflicting personalities without common goals? William Jones, president of Astrotek, a consulting firm dealing with high-technology processes, was having difficulties with one of his senior executives. During a discussion regarding the problem, Jones exclaimed, "I really hate coming to work and having to face Michaels." His agony was apparent, yet his behavior seemed strange. Why not transfer Michaels or, if need be, ask him to leave the company? When these alternatives were suggested, Jones retorted, "he has too much influence with the board."

Because the situation appeared irreconcilable, we were asked to undertake a careful examination of the organization. We interviewed all the key executives, and gave them the DSI. Then we asked them what roles they felt they would best fit in the company. Several important facts emerged. Jones was a right brain individual with very high conceptual and behavioral scores. His style was revealed by the fact that he allowed interruptions during important meetings and was unable to reprimand the individuals who caused the disruptions. His high need for acceptance (dominant behavioral style) kept him from confronting critical situations. His dominant conceptual style led him to expect very complete and elaborate reports, covering all the operations and planning in each of the divisions. When given a one-page report, he immediately rejected it as "incomplete, poor work, the executive failing to do his homework." Yet, with it all, Jones had had the vision to start the company, hire the key people, obtain contracts, and maintain solid growth in a highly technical company, even though his focus was not analytical and he had a very low directive score. Here was an individual who could write poetry, on the one hand, while building a major organization, on the other. The difficulties he encountered stemmed from his right brain orientation. He was too concerned about people's feelings, found confrontation difficult, and avoided major decisions, such as appointing key executives.

Jones was not alone in his frustration. Michaels, one of the senior executives at Astrotek, was an aggressive individual who wanted power and exercised considerable control. His dominant styles were analytical and behavioral; he had a low conceptual score. He was away from the office a great deal of the time and hired only people who had a strong analytical perspective. Of course, this was not strange, because the company was involved in highly technical work. However, Michaels clearly felt more comfortable with technical subordinates than he did with Jones. The conflict was inevitable. The two men saw the world from differing points of view, which they could not reconcile. Yet, without Jones's vision and risk taking, there would be no company at all. The question of how this situation could be rectified remained.

Following the interviews with the key executives and a review of their decision styles, we held a session with all of the company's executives to explore alternatives to the present organization structure. Decision style data from each key executive was considered, along with Jones's express objectives for the organization. The relationship between an individual's decision style and his or her outlook and concerns was clearly reflected in the remarks that they made about themselves during the interviews:

> *Executive A* (dominant analytical, backup behavioral): does not like hectic projects; prefers analysis, science, and ideas; rescues projects (an urgent requirement).
> *Executive B* (dominant analytical, backup behavioral): wants interesting work and recognition; values honesty and integrity; works independently; wants explicit goals

written down; likes control of work and quality; prefers technical work to administrative details.

Executive C (dominant conceptual, backup analytical): wants to feel important, to help others, to give people growth; sees both sides of issues but wants total control and wants to see the whole picture; is flexible and sees possibilities; suggests more rules and controls.

Executive D (dominant analytical, dominant behavioral): prefers person-to-person discussion rather than reports; will ask for written reports but allows independent action and delegation, management by exception; looks for details, bottom-line facts; values doers who are aggressive but not overbearing, who do not cover up, who are willing to work hard; expects alternatives for problems or otherwise will take charge and use own ideas; needs to control and will not give up responsibility too soon.

Executive E (dominant analytical, dominant directive, backup behavioral): looks for positive approach and alternatives in crisis; is sympathetic to others and gets along well; would like better communication with management; wants flexibility, guidelines, technically sophisticated projects with quality; feels that work is tedious and not up to expectations; values accuracy, quality, priority; consults with others when in doubt, avoids confrontation; would like more personal relations.

Executive F (dominant analytical, dominant conceptual, backup behavioral): wants more structure and definition in job functions; feels that there is too much ambiguity and that relations are too informal; is intuitive with people; feels that main pressure is lack of time; wants happiness in the job but enjoys accomplishing results; likes to organize, is willing to confront and be assertive.

Executive G (dominant analytical, backup directive, backup conceptual): prefers verbal response to written documents; has had disagreements with subordinates but resolves them quickly by joint discussion; gives rational answer; tries to do something but will not make promises that he cannot keep; expects subordinates to have loyalty, self-confidence, initiative, accept responsibility, and operate with guidelines; likes to see a good, complete job done; looks for recognition, challenge, growth, money; is willing to compromise, has difficulty convincing others, does not like to oversell.

Executive H (dominant analytical, dominant conceptual, dominant behavioral): feels that superiors should give broad guidelines; likes responsibility, delegates and trains subordinates; tries to avoid stress by keeping on top of things; looks for structure and logic in his job; expects results, worthwhile outputs, intellectually interesting work; is frustrated by inconsistencies when policies are not followed or people are not used effectively; prefers managing people to technical supervision.

Executive I (dominant behavioral, backup conceptual): would like to have more creative work, to give customers ideas; feels that her department gets projects that are in trouble; has difficulty communicating, has no interaction with the management committee; is willing to confront situations to straighten them out; wants direct verbal contact; has good insight or intuition in hiring people; is not willing to fight with superiors; likes project work, complicated problems, and results.

Executive J (dominant conceptual, backup analytical, backup behavioral): is concerned about morale; would motivate, help career development, improve writing, negotiations, and evaluations, and develop possibilities; is willing to put personal needs aside and look for new responsibilities; states that people come to him on a personal level to ask what is happening; uses systems approach, focuses on writing it down, and uses logic.

Executive K (dominant conceptual, dominant behavioral): enjoys interacting with a small group, shaping the group around a target, and achieving it; is frustrated at having to wear two hats—corporate and division; is desperate to have a target developed; seeks career goals, dedication, personal interaction; delegates responsibility and is frustrated when it does not work; in difficult situations, examines several aspects; does not like to order people around; will not confront.

Executive L (dominant conceptual, backup behavioral): prefers to plan ahead in a step-by-step approach with specific outlines and to avoid conflict and problems; cannot think effectively at office—takes work home; feels that there is a lack of organization and coordination; is willing to compromise; feels that there is not enough information; feels that an organization design is an iterative process that has to be made to work and that people should be willing to take risks.

A cursory review of the comments made by each executive and the match with style reveals a fairly consistent pattern. Embedded in the comments are reactions to the interview process, concerns about revealing information, uncertainty about how the information would affect them, and a genuine desire to ameliorate the situation. Given the amount of "noise" in the process, we can conclude that style is a reasonably accurate prediction of people's responses to organizational problems.

As might be suspected, any organizational structure is at best a compromise among the many factions and desires of individuals, mitigated by the environmental forces impinging on the organization, such as competition or technology.

Under the organizational structure in force when we began the discussion with Jones, two people, the director of personnel and Michaels, reported to the president. All division managers and directors reported to Michaels, with no direct interaction with the president. Under the new structure, which evolved out of a number of meetings with the key executives and with Jones, the divisions reported directly to Jones, and Michaels was given a new position that considered his needs and capabilities, as well as the requirements of the company. The company needed an individual who could develop new contacts and new products in order to sustain its current growth. Michaels was ideally suited for that job. At the same time, he now had less direct influence inside the company and less frequent contact with Jones. With the new organization structure, the division heads reported directly to Jones and he could interact with them and provide the direction that he felt the company needed while satisfying his own need as a conceptual behavioral.

From the initial meeting with Jones to the time that the final changes were made in the organization, the process took six months. Sessions were held to discuss the several proposed alternatives, and each individual executive was interviewed separately to determine his or her acceptance of the final proposal. Michaels accepted the new position, although he was somewhat reluctant to give up the power that he wielded internally. Only one other executive was concerned about the change, and she indicated that she would probably return to a company where the position was more "compatible" with her style. The transition was smooth, and the new structure has functioned in the new mode for a number of years.

Organizations are successful when they can build communities where styles match roles so that members are able to meet the challenges that they face and achieve personal satisfaction. Finding an appropriate match is a never-ending process and an important function of an executive. Some organizations achieve this alignment intuitively, as happened at Honda and Lotus. Others, such as Astrotek and Spectronics, try to determine an appropriate alignment by using a more systematic approach.

Spectronics Revisited. After his experience at Spectronics with Peter Oster, Tom Gardner became more attentive to the decision styles of his employees. The DSI was administered to key employees, and the language of style was used to discuss each personnel appointment before it was made. On one occasion, a disagreement flaired up between Don Pflug, the director of engineering, and Dave Martins, the newly promoted chief engineer. In the heat of an argument, both had threatened to quit. As a means of diffusing the argument, Gardner arranged for Martins to take the DSI and for Pflug to fill it out the way that he thought Martins would. Pflug incorrectly predicted Martins's responses on 50 percent of the questions. Obviously, Pflug did not understand Martins's needs.

Gardner used the results of the DSI to discuss the flair-up. First he met with Martins. Martins's style was dominant analytical, which is typical for engineering, and dominant behavioral, which accounted for his flairing up during an argument. His high behavioral score and his answer on the DSI regarding the need to feel secure prompted Gardner to ask, "Dave, do you feel secure in your job here?" Martins retorted, "I feel that I am going to be fired as soon as I finish my current project." Gardner asked, "Why would you have been promoted and why would I ask to talk to you if you were going to get fired?" This reassuring reaction was exactly what Martins needed. He wanted to feel secure in the job; he also disliked conflict with others and desperately wanted acceptance by the group. He had a strong need for affiliation, and his altercation with Pflug was threatening it. Once Martins felt assured that Gardner and the other executives supported him and appreciated his engineering skills, he calmed down and was able to go back to work. Martins was exceptionally good at solving problems, and this talent was needed to meet the company's expanding product lines. Over a three-year period, the value of Martins's contribution to the company was estimated at $5 million.

The meeting with Pflug did not go as well. As he had a dominant directive and dominant analytical style, it was not surprising that he had a reputation for poor interpersonal relationships. Gardner started by discussing Pflug's highly task, technical, and thinking orientation—an evaluation that he readily accepted. Gardner then suggested that this might account for his difficulty in understanding Martins, who was more behavioral. Pflug apparently misinterpreted this comment and began to talk about the absolute requirement for technical competence among the executives of a high-tech firm such as Spectronics. Pflug had proved his competence in his previous job as director of manufacturing and in other engineering positions. He had made valuable contributions to the firm's early products and production processes. But he had always had difficulty getting along with people. He now was having difficulty with the people in his department and was at loggerheads with other directors and his chief engineer, Martins. He seemed unable to understand that people had feelings; this was his intransigent shadow side. After some agonizing, Gardner finally suggested that Pflug find a new job. He did leave and found a position more closely matched to his analytical directive style, where he felt right at home.

Alignment is needed at all levels of an organization, as can be seen in the example of Betty Stapleton, who had joined the company as Gardner's secretary when he had just started. She was outgoing, warm, and friendly and became a sort of glue that held many of the interpersonal relationships in the company together. Her strong behavioral and conceptual scores helped to explain this. It was natural, then, for Gardner to appoint her director of personnel as the growth of the company led to a need for that position. At the outset, she worked out well, since the job consisted primarily of interviewing people and coordinating activities such as the company newsletter and the annual picnic. As the company grew, however, the job expanded to include administering compensation, insurance, and retirement plans and dealing with all of the legal aspects of industrial relations that a growing company faces. In addition, Stapleton was assigned responsibility for training the operating and managerial staff. Although she was very conscientious— people referred to her as bright, perceptive, and supportive— she simply was not able to handle all of these responsibilities. When her DSI scores were discussed with her, she acknowledged that administering benefit plans required analytical skills that she did not enjoy using. Further discussion showed that her strong behavioral style accounted for her fondness for training and other personnel activities. But she had to acknowledge that her background was not suited for the administrative and legal requirements of the job. After much soul searching, she returned to a senior secretarial job, where she was effective and happy until she left after a few years to have a child. An examination of Stapleton's case illustrates that decision style indicates an individual's preferences, not capabilities. Interestingly, except for the administration of the benefits packages—which could have been assigned to another person—Stapleton was stylistically fit for the job of director of personnel, but she lacked the requisite background skills. The language of style helped to address the problem but, given the context, there was not an acceptable alignment between her and her work requirements.

Arthur Bears represented still another kind of alignment at Spectronics. He was a delightful individual, friendly and pleasant and, as Gardner recounted, loyal and trustworthy. During a discussion on strategic planning, he was asked to identify three weaknesses of Spectronics. He was not able to utter a single word. He was then asked, "Can you name two?" Still no response. "Well, how about one?" More silence. He was truly unable to respond, because, as he said at another meeting, he felt that he might say something that would "put someone down." His dominant behavioral score was consistent with this concern for others. His strong behavioral style, however, proved to be a problem when he interacted with an outside consultant who had been contracted to convert the company's data-processing system. Month by month, the conversion fell behind schedule. Gardner and others expressed concern, but it was almost a year before Bears confronted the consultant and discharged him. He said that it was a "painful experience." A new consultant was hired, and with Bears's and others' concurrence, the conversion project was assigned to another manager, one who had a much higher directive score. Bears returned to dealing with his area of corporate finance, where his analytical style fit very well. Finance had been his responsibility from the start, and he continued to perform well in that job. After giving up the data-processing responsibility, his friendly smile and helpful hand returned.

Spectronics continues to be a successful and well-managed company. It has experienced all of the growing pains that any rapidly growing high-tech firm does; but it has overcome them and has flourished. As is true of any company, there have been false starts in some personnel assignments, and yet it has remained a profitable company. This is due, in large part, to Gardner's intuitive understanding of stylistic alignment. He has always sought a good fit between a person's interests and skills and

the requirements of a job. The DSI and the language of style
have become effective tools for him to use to accomplish this
objective, helping the company to understand people and how
they see themselves, and to seek successful marriages, like the
one Honda and Fujisawa formed and the one Kapor and Manzi
hoped to form. In short, the language of style has helped Spectronics form an effective community, one that provides a solid
basis for success and an ability to compete effectively in the
marketplace.

Style and Organizational Change

Why is introducing change in organizations such a difficult task? Every executive knows that organizations must continuously adapt to new environmental demands. Is it, perhaps,
that planning concentrates on the technical or financial requirements of change without due regard for organizational considerations? While many executives recognize the need to deal more
effectively with the change process, to correctly introduce change
or even to determine the likelihood of successful implementation is extremely difficult.

Illustrative of the requirement to change is the wave of
mergers that, more often than not, simply do not work. Studies
reported by Drucker (1987) indicate that one-half to two-thirds
of mergers turn out to be counterproductive and fall far short
of expectations. Even those mergers that seem to work often die
a slow death. In the face of such findings, why does merger mania
continue its strong hold on so many corporate executives? The
answer appears to be that excellence in management is not the
critical consideration when dealing with financial implications.
"Indeed, conflicting corporate cultures have been the undoing
of many acquisitions" (Rowe and Mann, 1986, p. 2), and attention is paid to firefighting and achieving financial objectives.

The sad reality is that many mergers should never have
taken place. Reports indicate that when Exxon spent over $600
million to acquire an office systems company, what started as
a great concept wound up as an implementation fiasco. Exxon's
purchase of Reliance Electric, with a price tag of some $1.2

billion, likewise proved unfortunate. Another such example is the sale of Synertek by Honeywell. Some former managers of Synertek grumbled that, rather than concentrate on the job, they had to constantly haggle over resources. The haggling was culturally unacceptable to these managers and led to many departures.

There is much criticism voiced about acquisition, the attractiveness of mergers, and their frequent failure. The arguments center on corporate culture, defined as the values, norms, and rituals of the organization as a whole. One large international consulting group insists that change cannot successfully be implemented without a careful consideration of corporate culture, because people often cling to their ingrained values, beliefs, and standards as to what they are willing to do, even when a logical analysis should convince them otherwise. What, then, should the executive do? Is corporate culture responsible for failures to introduce change? A question this complex defies a simple answer. While one may be able to identify which factors impede change, their impact is difficult to determine. Corporate culture is the very heart of an organization. Business is carried on within a cultural environment that develops and becomes self-perpetuating. The mores, values, norms, roles, and relationships that define a particular culture determine to a large extent the executive's ability to introduce change. The internal cultural environment of an organization, however, represents only a part of the story. External factors, notably important stakeholders—such as the banks, the federal government, or competitors—must also be considered when attempting to introduce organizational change. For example, the Chrysler Corporation in the throes of bankruptcy was able to convince the federal government that a loan to the company was in the best interest of the country. With this support, Lee Iacocca was able to bring a fresh and invigorating culture to Chrysler by exemplary leadership and a new management team. The results speak for themselves.

As most executives know, the introduction of change creates anxiety and fear. When a major change is in the offing as the result of some newly proposed strategy, fear and anxiety may cause high levels of "fight," "flight," or "freeze." A *Los Angeles Times* business headline read, "Wells Fargo Is Ready to Crack the Whip at Crocker" (1986). Wells Fargo chair Carl Reichardt is known for his relentless drive to cut costs. When Wells Fargo announced that it would pay $1.08 billion to buy Crocker from British Midland Bank, it was estimated that only ten out of the fifty top Crocker officers would remain and that as many as 100 of the combined 626 offices would be eliminated. The article stated, "The Crocker people must be very upset" (p. 1, 2). Managers will be confronted more and more with situations similar to the one at Crocker Bank. Style can provide guidance for alternative careers or clues to whether there is compatibility between employees and the new owners. In either case, the trauma of organizational change can be minimized if the consequences and alternatives are understood.

In order to make change effective, executives need to recognize that there is more to consider than the mere desirability of change. Four key factors have been identified that together determine the potential for successful change (Rowe and Mann, 1986): (1) the executive who is the change agent; (2) the corporate culture, which reflects the change environment; (3) the values and beliefs of the individual performers that affect the change process; and (4) the match, or fit, between the values of the individual performers and the corporate culture. This match determines whether the change is acceptable, the ease of change, and whether change will take place at all or become distorted or blocked.

The Change Agent. As a change agent, the executive reflects values that remain strong and dominate the culture. These values are a key aspect of the executive's decision style. Often, a founder's vision, building on a recognition of opportunities, needs, and requirements, is so strong and powerful that others "buy in" to that vision. In such a case, the company's direction is determined by the founder's preferences for the means of carrying out what the founder believes to be in the best interest of the company. The classic example is T. J. Watson at IBM. In his book *A Business and Its Beliefs* (Watson, 1963, p. 4), he states, "I believe the real difference between success and failure in a corporation can very often be traced to the question of how well the organization brings out the great energies and talents of its people.'' IBM has created an enduring culture that has made it a world leader in computers. Watson's vision and support of people still premeate the organization. He further stated that the single most important factor in success is the adherence to ''a sound set of beliefs.''

When the change agent introduces a change, it is critical that the organization is ready to follow and lend support. Although corporate culture at the top level may be supportive, it does not follow that the organization as a whole is ready to pursue the same goals. Members of the organization who must implement the change are often insulated from the dynamics at the top. While there are variations in the corporate culture at different levels of an organization, in many companies, such as IBM, there is a pervasive corporate culture. Howard Schwartz, a vice-president at Management Analysis Corporation, is actively involved with organizations dealing with changing culture. He has observed that if the chief executive is to be an effective change agent, any new direction should be identified in the context of the organization's core values and guiding beliefs. When changes are needed to facilitate implementation of a new direction, the change agent should:

1. Communicate knowledge about the need for change to meet forces in a competitive environment.
2. Develop a vision about the new direction that can be shared by members of the organization.
3. Determine what needs to be changed in beliefs, values, norms, structure, and protocol for the new direction to succeed.
4. Make the president's office the focal point of support for the proposed changes.
5. Formulate means to ensure that the changed culture is reinforced and supports the new direction.

To place the role of the change agent in proper perspective, one should consider the process needed to bring about

change. At the executive level of management, the time horizon
is projected into the future, and there is concern with long-term
survival of the company. For example, a study at General Electric showed that upper management spent 25 percent of their
time planning, while other studies indicate that first-line supervisors spend 45 percent of their time on matters with a one-day
horizon and 55 percent on matters with a one-month horizon.
Group vice-presidents and chief operating officers devote about
25 percent of their time to matters with a one-year horizon.
CEOs have a much longer-term planning horizon: about 70 percent of their time is concerned with a five-year outlook.

Corporate Culture. As was mentioned above, the change process
is ultimately dependent on corporate culture. The cultural environment is the sum total of shared values, attitudes, beliefs, norms,
rituals, structure, power centers, and assumptions of the people
involved in the change to be introduced. Terrence Deal and Allan
Kennedy (1984), in their best-selling book on *Corporate Cultures,*
observed that culture meets social needs by defining relationships,
specifying roles and duties, and establishing standards to be
followed. Rituals provide a means of demonstrating the values
and beliefs of the organization and thus define the culture, the
social interaction, the priorities, and the way individuals deal
with one another. At IBM, marketing drives a service philosophy. At ITT, financial discipline demands total dedication.
Digital Equipment Corporation creates freedom with responsibility by emphasizing innovation. Delta produces teamwork by
its focus on customer service. ARCO emphasizes entrepreneurship that encourages action. J. C. Penney considers long-term
loyalty more important than being an aggressive competitor.
These companies produce significant results in different fields,
all by adhering faithfully to a corporate culture that fits the
organization while helping to meet competitive challenges.

Values. The values held by those individuals who are expected
to implement the change comprise the third ingredient of the
change process. Some values are so ingrained and strongly held
that they can even be irrational. They can seriously inhibit or

prevent change. These must be understood and dealt with to assure commitment to a proposed change.

Values are the fundamental premises that we all use to judge what is important and what we believe in. They are intrinsic, deep-seated beliefs that are so pervasive that they influence every major decision we make—our moral judgments, reactions to others, willingness to make commitments, and support for organizational goals. Values determine what "really counts." The importance of values cannot be overestimated. They form a hidden source of strength, commitment, and dedication that goes way beyond normal incentives or rewards. In a study reported by Posner and Schmidt (1984) involving nearly 1,500 managers across the United States, they found that goals were seen as more important by those who felt that their values were consistent with the goals of the organization. Shared values lead to increased strength of commitment, a sense of success and fulfillment, a healthy perspective on work, and an understanding of the values and ethics of colleagues, subordinates, and management, along with a more positive attitude regarding organizational objectives and organizational stakeholders. Obviously, values alone do not make the difference; but where values of the individuals match the cultural values of the organization, there is a symbiosis—a fit that transcends almost any other form of relationship in an organization.

Fit. The concept of fit, then, is an important element in the change process. It is one of the most critical aspects of successful implementation. The acceptance of change has been called "the third level" by Sathe (1985), because implementation is a difficult process. This is precisely where the change process often breaks down. Not until the proposed change is accepted, internalized, and made a part of the values of those involved can the change take place and continue through to successful implementation.

The executive's decision style determines how effective a change agent he or she will be. As a change agent, the executive interacts with various internal and external cultures relevant to each situation. For change to be successful, then, the change agent's managerial style, the cultural environment's receptivity, and the strongly held beliefs and values of the individuals work best when they fit appropriately. The match between an individual's values and the cultural norms often determines the acceptability of the change and, ultimately, the likelihood of successful implementation. The function of the executive is to blend the individual's values with the cultural norms and to inspire individuals to accept ownership of the proposed change. By recognizing personal preferences in style, the executive can more effectively interact with subordinates in order to make a decision workable. A set of guidelines for dealing with preferences is shown below:

1. Understand an individual's preferences and biases and determine whether they "dominate" in any given situation.
2. Knowing that preferences will be used, assess their priority and determine how much weight to place on the needs of the individual.
3. Be sensitive to the styles and feelings of others. To ignore them is to invite conflict and even failure.
4. Listen to others' ideas. They may present the clue to their personal preferences and thus provide the basis that will make a situation workable.
5. When decisions appear irrational, personal preference may be the explanation and, perhaps, the basis for rectifying a bad situation.
6. Identify which factors are needed to motivate subordinates; for example, recognition, status, achievements.
7. Anticipate situations that may lead to conflict. Once a preference has been stated, it is often too late to change the individual's mind.
8. Recognize those factors that affect personal preferences: new conditions, a turbulent environment, political forces, or conflicting behaviors. Expect a shift in personal preference in response to the evolving situation.

Decisions made on the basis of personal preference are not necessarily bad, and indeed, when the decision maker has full discretion, personal preferences provide the basis for commitment to carrying out the decision. What we can learn from the examples covered is that "fit" extends beyond matching one's style to the job and the environment. Fit is also important in interpersonal relations, in managing and designing organizations, and in implementing change. Again, the language of style provides us with a valuable tool.

7

●II●II●II●II●II●II●II●II●II●II●II●II●II●II●II●II●II●II●II●II●II●II●II●II●II●II●II●II●

The Decision Style–Job Match:
Choosing Meaningful Careers

"What's wrong? Schuyler is the third top executive we've lost this year. We pay more than any company in the industry," the president of Consolidated Dynamics is saying. James Ackerman looks at the president thoughtfully. "Harold," he says at last, "I don't know how to tell you this, but you're a strong chief executive with very definite ideas on everything, and perhaps the people you have at the top are not being given the incentive to see what they can do. You reward them for carrying out your immediate plans, but not for the basic strategies that you have formally devised. I believe the three who left us felt stifled" (Cawly, 1986, p. 9). Even with the best of intentions, many companies are rewarding their top decision makers in ways that may not be best for the organization, and the companies themselves may not be receiving the full benefits of the executives' efforts and talents.

The owner of a highly successful real estate development company wanted to ensure the continuity of the business after his retirement. "I thought that a stock plan would give each executive an incentive to stay with the company and have our long-term interests in mind." Instead of promoting executive ownership of the company, he found that as soon as the stock was granted, it was cashed in. In another case, the management of a major *Fortune* 500 company recognized that it needed to diversify into other areas over the next five years. The company's president knew that the existing compensation plan was primarily geared to motivating executives to maintain annual earnings and not designed to implement long-term decisions. He candidly commented, "After all these years of motivating our executives to be short-term oriented, we did not realize how difficult it would be to get them to take the long-term view."

Looking at the management of organizations from a broad perspective, James O'Toole (1972, p. xv) in his book *Work in America* observed "a significant number of American workers are dissatisfied with the quality of their working lives." Their work, he went on to say, is dull and repetitive. They are given seemingly meaningless tasks, offering little challenge or autonomy. These concerns are causing discontent among workers at all occupational levels. When we consider the cost of both personal dissatisfaction and misplaced talent, it becomes obvious that there is considerable potential benefit in improving career planning, both for oneself and for members of the organization. Security Pacific National Bank has taken a significant step in overcoming the problem and has saved nearly $1 million in direct recruiting costs by searching for talent internally. Nearly 250 job openings, at salaries up to $43,000, are listed in a weekly internal publication, and more than 1,000 individuals have transferred within the organization. As a further incentive, employees are paid a bounty for referring qualified external candidates to the bank.

Concern has been expressed by Janis and Wheeler (1978) that too little thought is given to choosing a career. In their article on "Avoiding Career Mistakes," they refer to interviews with eighty-one middle-level executives of a large industrial organization. Many said that they were "disgusted" with their jobs. Their complaints centered around petty rules, dull routines, obstacles to promotion, long hours that interfered with home lives, and disruptions from continual reorganizations. What was most significant about their complaints were the regrets about the decision to come to work for the company. They admitted that they should have found out more about the work before accepting the job. These same complaints are voiced by lawyers, physicians, and other technical specialists.

Drucker (1987) voiced concern over a growing mismatch between jobs and those seeking jobs. Not only are individuals unprepared for many of the emerging technologies, but their aspirations and expectations suggest that advancement comes through managerial rather than professional careers. Drucker suggests that to bridge the gap, we will have to both change expectations and redesign jobs so that they will remain challenging and rewarding over the long haul. He goes on to say that with the ability of workers to shift from one job to another, employers will have to "design" jobs so that they become attractive to prospective employees. This suggests a greater need to understand employees so that a better match can be achieved between people and jobs.

The mismatch of personality and jobs can be devastating, as observed by Harry Levinson (1978), who found that an abrasive personality is the single most frequent cause for the failure of bright men and women in the executive ranks of business and industry. Levinson said that this kind of person, "who, like the proverbial porcupine, seems to have a natural knack for jabbing others in an irritating, sometimes painful, way" (p. 78), unconsciously undermines his or her success and is usually either fired by an exasperated boss or stuck permanently at the lower levels of the company. The abrasive personality, often reflecting a directive/analytical style, "frequently criticizes others, often to a bruising point and with little diplomacy," Levinson said. "He characteristically questions, analyzes and demolishes his colleagues' positions, sometimes even provokes their hostility. His penetrating insight [analytical style] is often undermined and vitiated by the condescending manner [low behavioral] in which he offers his views. He has little capacity for diplomacy, is rarely able to sense other people's feelings by putting himself in their shoes, and frequently insists that he must be 'open,' 'truthful,' and 'tell it like it is'" (p. 78).

Why do intelligent, well-educated people make poor career choices, and how might they avoid their mistakes? It is clear that few individuals are very aware of their potential and their strong preferences and that most tend to make career choices opportunistically rather than using a systematic plan. Given that our self-image is shaped by the work that we do, a healthy approach would be for each individual to build on his or her distinctive strengths and preferences. Although, in years past, having a job at all was important, now the concern is: How can I be myself and also do what I am best at? How can we utilize style as a means for matching people with job requirements? Brousseau (1983) has suggested that to achieve a job-person fit, factors such as the following should be considered: (1) the organization's philosophy and norms regarding employee participation in decision making; (2) the relative scarcity of jobs; (3) the degree to which abilities and preferences match available jobs; and (4) the way in which human resource specialists determine job fit, as well as the consequences of job movement and training.

Obviously, decision style–job match alone will not determine either the level of satisfaction or the opportunity to succeed in a given organization. Rather, the style–job match provides the basis on which to build a career, because a poor fit will almost certainly assure failure, regardless of the organization in which one works. In a study of more than 11,000 top executives, Swinyard and Bond (1980) found a number of important factors that affect promotions from the level of vice-president to that of president. Individuals who are promoted tend to have a better education than the people they are replacing, and a large percentage have advanced degrees in business administration. The new executives generally are not any younger than the people they replace and generally have had prior experience as a group vice-president. Executives now have greater mobility because of more opportunities and their better educational backgrounds. Our data on presidents who have advanced degrees show that they have a higher tolerance for ambiguity and a broader perspective (combination analytical/conceptual) than a specialist who is advanced to higher positions in the firm solely on the basis of performance.

What about a person who is not promoted? Should that person quit or perhaps choose a second career? Levinson (1983) identifies as the most critical factor for people considering a second career an understanding of their ego ideal, which deals with their ''real aspirations'' concerning their future. He considers attaining one's ego ideal as the most powerful motivating force in determining which occupation best fits one's personality, attraction to a given job, and interaction with other workers. Here again, decision styles provide valuable insight into what a person would find most satisfying. Artists tend to dislike math. Teachers enjoy working with people. Engineers enjoy the challenge of solving complex new designs, and salespeople have the drive needed to get an order or to close a deal. As Levinson suggests, once we understand who we are, what we prefer, and what opportunities are available, we are in a better position to find a job-personality match rather than merely accepting whatever job comes along. The premise is that a good job fit or, as we have termed it, "alignment" should provide greater satisfaction because of the reinforcement gained by doing a job well. We often see people, such as computer programmers, work all night on a tricky problem to have the satisfaction of solving it.

Because the four basic styles and the style patterns give us clues as to what we would enjoy doing, it is quite natural that there would be a close relationship between what type of position a person would find meaningful and his or her scores on the Decision Style Inventory. When we asked a number of technically oriented presidents, engineers, accountants, and lawyers who had high conceptual scores why they had shifted to management from their technical specialties, invariably the response was the preference for greater freedom that a managerial role provided. The converse situation was observed in an instance where the senior partner in a law firm had been asked to prepare a long-range plan concerning the future direction of the company. He felt very "uncomfortable" with the assignment, in part because of his dominant analytical style, typical of attorneys. He had a very low conceptual score and simply could not bring himself to look out into the unknown and define a "new direction" for the firm. He clearly recognized what his preferred activities would be. A basic premise underlying style is that people do know themselves but need a language to express who they are. The classification and interpretation of the DSI match very well how people see themselves.

Women Executives and Careers

When W. Ann Reynolds was appointed chancellor of the California State University, a question was raised: Was she nominated because she was a woman or because of her capabilities? She was known for having the ability to work hard, for meeting problems head on, for making tough decisions, for being very bright, and for being a "quick studier and a doer." Indeed, it was these attributes, usually ascribed to men rather than women, that convinced the board of trustees to appoint Reynolds. Three years after her appointment, there was serious opposition from the board, who felt she spent too much time away, was a poor administrator, and frequently berated subordinates in public. Her highly directive style, which emphasized working hard and achieving results, was causing problems. This was a case of misalignment. While Reynolds was obviously a very capable person, the university board of trustees was not receptive to her talents and focused on what they considered her shortcomings. In another setting, Reynolds's hard driving style would be appreciated and rewarded.

Marcia Israel, president and chief executive of Judy's, Inc., and creator and president of Golden Goose Electronics, Inc., was chosen as the recipient of the Outstanding Entrepreneur of the Year Award in 1983. Israel has proved that there are no boundaries to entrepreneurial success for a leading woman in the retailing business. Judy's has grown from seventeen stores in 1972 to a present seventy-two stores, spanning Southern and Northern California, Arizona, New Mexico, Nevada, and Texas. In addition to a large selection of women's apparel, Judy's has men's departments, called "Gear for Guys," which sell pants, shirts, sports coats, and various accessories for men. Golden Goose Electronics is profitably producing a highly technical system to deter and detect shoplifting.

Why, then, are women thought of as being different from men in terms of their ability to perform effectively in management positions? Perhaps this notion persists because of studies such as the one at Johns Hopkins that claimed that there are significant differences in mental functioning between men and women—despite a persistent doubt about the validity of such studies. In that study, men were described as excelling in numerical reasoning and spatial judgment, while women were considered superior in verbal fluency and rote memory. Social, cultural, and environmental influences were discounted, and differences between men and women were attributed to their levels of androgens (male hormones), which are generally associated with aggressive or assertive behavior. The study claimed that females with high levels of androgens were more likely to excel in math and to be as aggressive as men are supposed to be.

Where does the truth lie? Do physiological factors account for differences, or do personality factors, such as being assertive or having interpersonal skills, account for the way in which women think, perceive, behave, and react to their job demands? Research seems to show that decision styles—ways of perceiving and understanding information—play a dominant, if not overriding, role in determining how individuals respond to stimuli, solve problems, interact with others, and make decisions or choices.

We compared the DSI scores of women in technically oriented occupations with those of women in socially oriented work; there is a significant difference between the decision styles of the two groups, as shown in Table 6. However, there was no real difference in style between women and men in the same fields. This study compared fifty-three women in technical fields, such as finance, accounting, law, sales, and real estate, with forty-six women who were pursuing careers in psychology, nursing, education, and art. The choice of career clearly reflects differences in style. The principal difference between these two

Table 6. DSI Scores of Women in Different Fields.

	Directive	Analytical	Conceptual	Behavioral
Technical	75	93	80	52
Social	66	78	85	71

groups is that the women who work in socially oriented fields have lower directive scores and much higher behavioral scores than women who work primarily in technical fields. Social professions tend to demand stronger conceptual and behavioral styles, while women in technical professions demonstrate stronger analytical and directive styles.

Do men and women have different styles? Our studies suggest that, on the whole, women tend to score slightly higher on behavioral styles than men. This, however, depends on the jobs that they prefer. Successful women have styles similar to those of successful men who hold the same kinds of jobs. Rowe and Boulgarides (1983) found only slight differences between the styles of 94 female business managers and 194 male managers. The principal difference was the shift from conceptual to behavioral for this sample of women. These data are shown in Table 7. Supporting this finding was a study of female

Table 7. Comparison of DSI Scores of Male and Female Managers.

	Directive	Analytical	Conceptual	Behavioral
Female managers	75	88	74	64
Male managers	74	89	83	54

engineers that showed that their values were closer to those of male engineers than to the values of women who were not in engineering. Thus, it is clear that many women have decision styles, personalities, values, and behaviors that are closer to those of their male counterparts than to the stereotype of the female population.

In another study, a comparison of 93 female managers and 224 female architects showed significant differences, as seen in Table 8. The data from this study show that female managers

Table 8. Comparison of DSI Scores of Female Managers and Architects.

	Directive	Analytical	Conceptual	Behavioral	Average Age
Female managers	73.5	87.5	74.4	64.2	40.2
Female architects	66.4	94.2	84.8	54.5	35.6

have higher directive and behavioral scores than female architects, who are more analytical and conceptual. These results are consistent with what one might expect. The manager's job involves more direction and dealing with people, whereas the architect's job involves analysis and creativity.

Comparisons Among Male Executives

A natural question one might ask is whether the same relationship holds for male executives as for female. Our data show that, in general, the occupation that one chooses is most often closely related to our style. A right brain individual will typically avoid occupations involving mathematics or science. This would not be the case for persons who are both right and left brain. Thus, we have found that medical technicians, for example, have higher behavioral and conceptual scores than the general population. This is the same conclusion that we observed when comparing women in technical and nontechnical occupations.

The data from a comparison of senior male executives with male engineering managers in a technical organization (shown in Table 9) reveal that senior executives had moderate analytical scores and high conceptual scores, while engineers had a higher than average analytical score, which is what one would expect. The senior executives had combined analytical and conceptual scores that were higher than average. In Chapter Three we defined this as the executive style in which both left and right brains apply.

Table 9. Comparison Among Selected U.S. Male Managers.

	Directive	Analytical	Conceptual	Behavioral
Senior executives	72	90	91	47
Male engineers	72	95	80	53

In a study by Richard Mann (1982), he compared the styles of male financial planners with those of male strategic planners, all of whom were considered to be proficient in their jobs. He discovered a sharp difference in style, as shown in Table 10. An examination of their scores reveals the distinctive nature of each of the jobs that might be accounted for by the differences in style. Financial planners must formulate problems, plow through large amounts of financial data, and perform detailed analyses. Their job requires a rather logical, systematic, and decisive turn of mind. Strategic planners, on the other hand,

Table 10. Comparison of Financial and Strategic Planners.

	Directive	Analytical	Conceptual	Behavioral
Financial planners	75	100	74	51
Strategic planners	62	81	100	57

must envision a much more varied and complex world. They must be facile with new ideas about the business, its direction, its products, and its markets. Their task requires a much more intuitive and creative perspective. The highly significant differences between the scores of these two groups for the directive, analytical, and conceptual styles reflect this difference in the demands of the jobs and also suggest that these thirty individuals were well suited for their work.

The fit between style and position is revealed in a study by Boulgarides and Rowe (1984) covering 150 police chiefs in the State of California, which concluded that police chiefs' styles were similar to those of senior executives. This shows how a stereotype can often be misleading. The data are shown in Table 11. This study was initially undertaken to determine whether chiefs of

Table 11. Comparison of Police Chiefs with Senior Business Managers.

	Directive	Analytical	Conceptual	Behavioral
Police chiefs	71	90	81	58
Senior executives	70	90	93	47

police had a style that suited them to operate effectively in an increasingly complex environment characterized by advanced communications technology, sophisticated crime detection procedures, and a new emphasis on the legal rights of citizens. The analysis of their style indicates that chiefs of police are as well suited for their work as are American business managers, who must also function in a complex environment. If anything, the chiefs' slightly higher behavioral scores and higher directive scores suggest that they have more concern for people and are less authoritarian than their business counterparts. Their profile indicates that, in general, they are sensitive to the needs of citizens.

Some professions require specific style profiles for success on the job. In a study that compared styles of admirals in the U.S. Navy with those of senior executives, the results were as shown in Table 12. It is clear that admirals are highly proficient at analytical tasks in their role as senior officers. Senior

Table 12. Comparison of Admirals and Executives.

	Directive	Analytical	Conceptual	Behavioral
Admirals	59	102	92	47
Senior executives	70	90	93	47

executives show a greater emphasis on results and entrepreneurial orientation. Their high conceptual scores indicate that both groups can deal effectively with broad thinking, vision, and creativity.

A Real Estate Case

Is there a magic formula for selecting and retaining top producers? Exploring this question, Trowbridge and Norris (1981) found that personality traits provided the clues needed to identify the top producers in real estate. They formulated the following personality profile of the typical successful real estate professional, in terms of ten factors.

1. Personal approval: is positively stimulated by recognition; is sensitive to own and others' behavior; seeks respect and recognition; is serious and trusting.
2. Group approval: gains positive self-image from group approval; is friendly; communicates easily; likes people.
3. Control: projects leadership and security; exerts influence; is self-assertive; prefers to lead; is competitive and aggressive.
4. Possessions: reinforces recognition by rewards; is motivated by material possessions; is competitive and resourceful.
5. Challenge: gains ego satisfaction from challenge; sets high goals; is committed and steadfast; likes to help; recognizes own shortcomings.

6. Order: likes predictability; is systematic and definite; follows through; uses rules and follows details.
7. Change: likes creativity and new ideas; is enthusiastic; accepts new assignments; is positive; is results oriented.
8. Decision making: uses data to solve problems; is careful; tries multiple solutions; plans ahead; uses past experience; knows consequences.
9. Activity: is typically a high-energy person; works hard; is persuasive; is competitive; sticks to personal beliefs.
10. Individuality: needs to be different; is creative; has ideas; likes freedom, independence and spontaneity; is individualistic.

If we recast these ten factors into decision style categories, we would find:

Factors	*Equivalent Decision Style*
1. Personal approval	Conceptual
2. Group approval	Behavioral
3. Control	Directive
4. Possessions	Directive
5. Challenge	Conceptual
6. Order	Directive
7. Change	Conceptual
8. Decision making	Analytical
9. Activity	Directive
10. Individuality	Conceptual

Although this matching is only approximate, it shows that a combination of conceptual and directive styles is characteristic of the most successful real estate brokers.

We analyzed the decision style scores of the top producers at the Los Angeles division of a major real estate firm, a large company that specialized in relatively exclusive and higher-priced residential property. Their clients expected much more from their brokers than the average home buyer, in part because the typical price of a house was a half million dollars or more. In this kind of business environment, a successful broker has to be self-reliant and assertive. Brokers who are unable to close a deal because they lack the ability to be assertive either let the client control the progress of the sale or else waste their time. Because both the price and the commissions are very high, the buyer and the seller both have to be convinced that they are making the right decision. This requires considerable gentle guiding and steering of the parties in order for the broker to make a sale. Once a contract is signed, there is still more work to do. It starts with obtaining all of the specific facts of the deal and being sure that they are handled correctly in escrow and properly recorded. Then come loan approvals and follow-ups on inspections.

All of these activities require a directive style. Of the forty-eight brokers in that office who took the DSI, twenty-nine scored above average on the directive scale, and twenty-five had dominant directive scores. Twenty-five of the brokers had both behavioral and directive styles. This combination is needed for the empathy needed in those inevitable "hand-holding" situations during difficult transition periods. A clue as to the utility of the behavioral style came from one of the managers. She said, "Purchasing a house is probably the single biggest decision people make in their life and one of the most emotional. This means that the broker has to be attentive to even the smallest personal need to make sure that the deal goes through. Some million-dollar deals have been squelched simply because of an argument as to who would keep the clothes washer or because the buyer did not like the seller's personality." These are the kinds of problems that the behavioral style tends to deal with well. The DSI was administered again three years later to the same group of brokers. During that three-year period, ten brokers had left the firm. Some of the individuals who left were good brokers and took jobs with other firms. Others were poor performers and dropped out of the business. The majority in the latter category scored low in the directive style.

An important aspect of real estate is that all earnings are based on commission. If there are no sales, there are no commissions. Without an advance on sales, brokers have to survive purely on what they earn. Those who make it do so by dint of persistence rather than just skill. Clients trust them and often send them referrals. These competent and skillful brokers almost invariably are directive in style. A particular case at this firm illustrates the need for fit. One of the young brokers was a relative of the manager. She joined the company because she was familiar with it. Her first two years in the business, however, proved less than satisfactory. The DSI revealed that she had a very dominant conceptual style and a very low directive. In a consultation with the manager, it was suggested that her style and interests pointed toward a career in the arts or acting. After a few more months of mediocre performance, she left the firm for a position in theater arts. Today she is doing well in theater arts, which seem to provide a better alignment for her style.

In a study of one of the two top-producing divisions in the country, we found that the truly outstanding producers had a combination directive and conceptual style. This confirms the Trowbridge findings and lends credence to the use of style as a predictor of success in one's career. But what about those brokers who were primarily action oriented, the directive/behavioral group? Our data suggest that, while many successful producers use that style, the truly outstanding ones have the conceptual/directive style. The reality is that in most organizations, only a small percentage of any occupational group are the very top performers. Thus, organizations seeking only the truly outstanding may be pursuing an unrealistic personnel goal; individuals may be successful in real estate without necessarily being at the very top in their field.

Spotting the Potentially Successful Executive

Companies try to spot individuals with potential early and then guide them to the top. NCR of Dayton, Ohio, though not seeking astronauts, is continuously looking for young employees who can "soar into the executive stratosphere." Hugh Stephenson, director of career planning and development at NCR, combed the records of 4,000 young employees and selected 828 whose performance was considered high. These employees were then asked to complete a biographical questionnaire and a psychological exercise. On the basis of these instruments, the company interviewed and tested approximately 100 candidates. They finally found 24 whom they considered high-potential employees. *Fortune* has been touting the return of personality tests as a basis for providing guidance in assigning executives to appropriate positions.

To identify candidates for key jobs at Sun Company, managers compiled dossiers on their 150 executives and interviewed subordinates, peers, and superiors to obtain firsthand impressions of the individuals. During the interviews, they asked questions about the candidates such as: How do they react to situations that do not go well? Are they strong conceptually? Are they able to see the big picture? Do they get bogged down in details? What do they stand for? While in many cases, the responses confirmed what had already been known, they provided an objective appraisal that supported the promotion decision. Our experience with the DSI has been similar. In several cases, the recommendations based on the DSI coincided exactly with the assessment made by top management. The value of the DSI was to reassure them that their decisions were, in fact, correct from the perspective of fit or alignment between style and job requirements.

In an interview with three executive search firms, it was ("The Right Executive . . . ," 1986) reported that one chief executive officer of a major corporation said that the "best" manager can pick the right person for the job only 75 percent of the time. This leaves quite a margin for error when someone less able than the best manager makes a judgment decision on hiring. Executive search firms recognize the difficulty of using a resumé as the basis for a hiring decision. They attempt to determine whether the individual shares the value system and culture of the company. They realize the importance of having "realistic" expectations and taking into account both objective data and subjective observations about the human element. We saw this in the real estate case, where there were few "ideal" brokers but many successful performers. In several organizations where the DSI is employed, it has been a meaningful supplement to the usual interview process, reference checks, and resumé data. The DSI is able to delve behind the facade of job titles, degrees held, or position descriptions. It relates the candidate to the position in a career-matching sense, thus providing greater assurance of successful performance on the job and as a member of the organization.

Style and Career Planning

Perhaps the most significant finding in our examination of career planning is that few executives follow a single career path. This is not really surprising when one considers the differences in style among individuals and the large number of possible style patterns. We have observed that for any given style pattern, there are easily ten to fifteen job categories that would match it. For example, consider the following pattern: directive 83 (dominant), analytical 87 (backup), conceptual 89 (dominant), behavioral 41 (least preferred). Positions that could match this pattern include senior executive, legal profession, education profession, design engineer, medical profession, graphic design, computer systems analyst, space systems engineer, photographer, biologist, economist, writer, financial analyst, and accountant. These job categories are by no means the only ones that would fit the style shown. They do clearly illustrate, however, the wide range of jobs that an individual with such a pattern could find satisfying. Now consider a second possible pattern: directive 94 (very dominant), analytical 52 (least preferred), conceptual 84 (backup), behavioral 70 (dominant). Positions that would match this pattern include general manager, medical specialist, education professional, supervisor, field director, recreation director, project scheduler, procurement analyst, social service worker, clinical psychologist, computer operator, dental hygienist, and nurse. Our approach in matching jobs with patterns was first to determine the characteristics of a given pattern and then to relate them to the requirements of a number of jobs. Many of the basic pattern studies were part of the validation of the DSI and involved sampling specific occupational groups, such as engineers or accountants.

How does one successfully choose a career once one's decision style is known? The answer involves several steps:

1. Start by determining one's decision style.
2. Look for a match with style patterns. Generally, this requires a computer search because of the large number of possible patterns. Otherwise, use the general approach that follows.
3. Determine whether one is primarily left brain or right brain.
   a. Left brain, or logical, people prefer occupations that involve analysis, numerical reasoning, problem solving, achieving results, being in control, and being able to focus mentally on the work to be done.
   b. Right brain people prefer occupations that involve people, require intuition or creativity, involve visual perspective or broad thinking, and include writing, artistic, or musical skills, and they are less focused in their thinking.
4. Determine whether one is primarily idea or action oriented.
   a. Idea-oriented people are more concerned with analysis, perspective, judgment, visualizing, innovation, creativity, music, art, writing, and new approaches.
   b. Action-oriented individuals are concerned with achieving results. They work well with others and find occupations that require direct involvement, achieving results, athletics, and interacting with the public.
5. Next, examine the level of dominance in each style to establish the style pattern. Look for occupations with greater or lesser requirements for the characteristics for individual styles and for left/right brain or idea/action orientation. In general, even a crude evaluation tends to provide valuable insights into career possibilities.

Now that a person's proclivity for certain occupations is determined, the next step is the choice of a job. Here, many external factors prevail, such as availability of openings, geographical location, kind of industry or company, pay level, opportunity for advancement, and so on. Our contention is that, given the mobility in today's society, a reasonably large number of occupations can match an individual's style. Alignment is concerned with matching a person's style with the specific requirements of a given job in a company. With the large number of possible jobs and the many specific requirements, it would be virtually impossible to precisely plan one's career ahead of time. Even occupations such as medicine, education, and the military, which might seem quite steadfast, are subject to change within the occupation that is tantamount to a change in job. For example, a teacher who becomes a principal or a military person who is assigned to new duties or a new location experiences a job change. Although low-skill jobs, such as janitor or sweeper, might remain reasonably constant throughout a person's career, this is seldom true in the life of an executive. Almost by definition, moving up the ranks to an executive position requires a constant shift of jobs. Similarly, moving from one industry to another or from one company to another requires new skills, new interactions, and new expectations. The planning of one's career, then, is not so much defining the path as establishing the goal and having the requisite competencies to achieve that goal. For some the goal might be power, for others prestige, for others wealth, and for still others challenge, opportunity, or quality of working life.

What style can do for career planning is help to avoid pitfalls and blind alleys. It can point the direction of possible alternative occupations and help to determine when there is an appropriate job match. With economists estimating that 25 percent of the labor force will become ''contingent'' workers— those who work at home, as contractors, or as volunteers—the need for match can become even more critical for organizations attempting to retain highly skilled professionals, such as attorneys or computer analysts. Style provides an objective basis on which individuals and companies can make more intelligent choices in career planning.

8

●ll●ll●ll●ll●ll●ll●ll●ll●ll●ll●ll●ll●ll●ll●ll●ll●ll●ll●ll●ll●ll●ll●ll●ll●ll●ll●ll●ll●ll●ll●ll●ll●ll●ll●ll●

Decision Styles
and Characteristics
of Executives, Leaders,
and Entrepreneurs

The Executive Style

A question often asked is whether executives, leaders, and entrepreneurs are different from each other. Most executives and leaders that we have studied have styles that overlap those of the entrepreneur. The pattern most frequently observed among the senior executives—chairpersons, CEOs, and presidents—is the "entrepreneurial" style, while vice-presidents and director-level executives tend to be more staff oriented; that is, the analytical/conceptual style dominates among them. As a group, the director level does not have a strong directive style. Leadership embodies a dominant conceptual style along with a behavioral backup. Thus, the conceptual style is the link among four executive patterns: (1) senior executive: *conceptual*/directive/analytical; (2) staff executive: analytical/*conceptual*; (3) leader: *conceptual*/behavioral/directive; (4) entrepreneur: *conceptual*/directive.

Over 79 percent of the eighty senior executives that we studied scored above the norm in the conceptual category, and 47 percent scored above the norm in the directive categoy. A kind of dreamer-realist picture emerges that matches the entrepreneurial style. Considering specific categories, 59 percent of the CEOs and chairpersons and 62 percent of the presidents had the entrepreneurial style. The executive first conceives of a new idea by reflecting on a number of considerations and responding to intuitive feelings. Then there is a shifting of mental images as he or she moves the idea into reality. Decisions are made, actions are taken, and reflection is short-circuited for a while. Upon completion of the detailed tasks, however, the executive then needs to stop, step back, and evaluate and reconceptualize the directions and plans. A new strategy is charted, and then it is back into the directive mode, with its sequential attention to tasks and the making of the decisions necessary to transform the ideas into reality.

Leaders, as Bennis and Nanus (1985) discovered in their study of executives, display four main areas of competency, all related to skills required to interact effectively with others. Among the skills that helped them succeed, first and most important was the ability to create a vision of new possibilities—the conceptual. Leaders had the ability to identify future directions that were exciting and compelling. This competency was supported by the ability to give the vision meaning through effective communication—the behavioral. Leaders must gain people's trust through persistence and positioning so that they can mobilize the power necessary to bring their vision into being—the conceptual. Because of their positive self-regard, leaders can accomplish results that others cannot—the directive.

The traits identified by Bennis and Nanus were revealed in extensive interviews with ninety leaders, including those from both the public and the private sector. In a survey of companies identified by *Forbes* magazine as the "up and comers," 92 percent of the chairpersons and 84 percent of the presidents had dominant conceptual styles. Of those surveyed, well over 75 percent had above-average scores in the directive category (Kichen, 1984). In our study of styles of successful senior executives, we found similar characteristics (see Table 13). Senior executives showed a much higher conceptual style than the typical American business manager. Their conceptual style is one that executives employ to find new and creative approaches to attaining future goals. They are able to create new visions, at the same

Table 13. Comparison of Senior Executives with the General Population.

	Senior Executives	General Population	Difference
Directive	75	75	None
Analytical	86	90	Executives less analytical
Conceptual	91	80	Executives more conceptual
Behavioral	47	55	Executives less behavioral

time focusing on the details necessary to make their visions a reality. The conceptual executive also prefers group discussions as the means for communicating. And the conceptual achieves positive self-regard by undertaking tasks that allow independent action and provide personal recognition.

Case Study: A Real Estate Developer

When we asked one of the senior executives that we interviewed, a real estate developer, what makes an excellent executive, he responded, "You have to be both a dreamer-generalist and a detail manager-realist. Executives must deal with the most far-reaching and unknown parts of their business while at the same time, they often must attend to the smallest details. My staff are the people who take care of everything in between."

To punctuate his point, the developer cited an example gleaned from his experience in building a new shopping mall in the Pacific Northwest, at the time of its construction among the largest in the world. He spoke fondly of how creativity was involved. He had conceived the overall plan, drawn sketches to share with architects, and designed a marketing strategy to entice retailers to join him. Throughout the life of the project, he said, he had felt the need to keep his "dream" in the minds of a large number of people—bankers, retailers, builders, and so on—and had succeeded. This, he argued, is one of the primary responsibilities of the chief executive. He found, however, that there was another responsibility. As the project progressed, he was required to make decisions and take action on many small details that were called to his attention. There were decisions regarding fixtures, plumbing, electrical outlets, facings, and so on, some of which were ultimately crucial to the success of the project as a whole. The vast majority of these decisions were made by architects, contractors, and foremen, but there were many details that he felt he had to attend to personally.

This need for specific, focused attention was illustrated by an event that took place one day while he was at the project site reviewing progress. His secretary notified him that one of the office staff was complaining of nausea and planned to go home before some of the executive's correspondence could be typed. As the secretary asked for his guidance on how to deal with the remaining work, she found that she too was feeling ill. She had hardly mentioned it to the executive when another employee came through the door on the way to the restroom to vomit. The executive hurried back to the office. When he arrived, he was met by another member of the office staff, who notified him that she was submitting a grievance to the labor union. "On what grounds?" he asked. "Because the new draperies in the office are making everyone sick," she replied. It was one of those ironic reversals that all executives must learn to live with. With the aid of a decorator, he had remodeled the office to make it more cheerful and pleasant. The new draperies, which matched the room's decor, had a plastic backing, which gave them sound-absorbing and insulating properties. As the executive was reviewing the situation, he received a call from a union representative. It was official. A formal complaint had been lodged.

During the next several weeks, he recalls, he became a mini-expert on the physiological effects of drapery odors. The puzzling question was whether the new draperies, which indeed gave off a slight odor, were responsible for the nausea or whether the illness was due to a virus or other cause. The answer carried enormous implications for his firm and its ability to keep the shopping mall project on schedule. Several scientists were called in, and the executive recalls crawling on the floor with them and with the union representative to conduct various tests on the draperies, carpets, and other new materials in the office. Their diligent efforts showed that there was no relationship between the new decorative materials and the reported illness.

Finally, after a public health official noted that there had been an increase in the incidence of influenza during that period, the union's complaint was dropped. The executive was then able to devote his full attention to the shopping mall project.

In summarizing his experience, the executive likened it to the maxim from Benjamin Franklin's *Poor Richard's Almanac:* A little neglect may breed great mischief . . . for want of a nail the shoe was lost, for want of a shoe the horse was lost, for want of the horse the rider was lost, and it goes on to the loss of battles and kingdoms. "Chief executives must deal with both the battles and with the nails," this executive concluded. "In the nail department one must have a 'decisive presence' and be able to respond quickly and effectively in order to establish control over a project and to keep it on target."

Other Profiles of Executives

The profile identified by the developer fits closely with the one that Robert L. Katz (1955) identified in his classic 1955 *Harvard Business Review* article "Skills of an Effective Administrator." Katz, a chief executive as well as an educator, argued that effective administration calls for a "conceptual skill" that he described as "involving the ability to see the enterprise as a whole; including recognizing how the various functions of the organization depend on one another, and how changes in any one part affect the others; and it extends to visualizing the relationship of the individual business to the industry, community and the political, social, and economic forces of the nation as a whole." This conceptual skill must be bolstered by supporting "technical skills" that provide "an understanding of, and proficiency in, a specific kind of activity, particularly one involving methods, processes, procedures or techniques" (Katz, 1955, p. 33). In a retrospective commentary on the 1955 article, Katz observed that the technical skills were probably more important than he had originally thought. Thirty years of additional work with company presidents and his own personal experience as a chief executive led him to conclude that, the effective executive must be able to efficiently deal with operating problems and strategic concerns. Our finding that the majority of CEOs have a conceptual/directive style suggests that they are well matched to their job as Katz described it.

A number of studies support the conceptual/directive nature of executive style and also augment our picture of the excellent executive. Grimsley and Jarrett (1973) pored over thousands of assessment records of managerial performance that they had collected during a twenty-year period. The results of their study showed that high levels of cognitive complexity and tolerance for ambiguity—traits that are shared among our conceptuals and analyticals—yielded an intellectual competence that was correlated with success at upper levels of management. The personality measures that they used were space visualization, perceptual speed, fluency, verbal comprehension, reasoning, and facility with numbers. Their correlations were sufficiently high to conclude that these personality measures would potentially be good predictors of who would be an effective manager.

In another study of the relationship between personal characteristics and occupational success, Wald and Doty (1954) employed a combination of tests and interviews to obtain a "complete" case history of executives. Their findings elaborate the executive profile. Their early family life, nationality, socio-economic status, and relations within the family are significant determinants of their personal development. Executives' parents have above-average educational levels. More than half of their fathers were in professional or managerial occupations, and 67 percent graduated from college. Executives' intellectual ability ranked higher than that of 96 percent of the population of business and industrial workers. The two dominant personality characteristics were firmness and frankness, manifested by their being forceful, intense, willing to take risks, and ambitious. Other important factors included persuasiveness and literacy, which promoted harmonious human relations in dealing with people.

In a survey of 492 presidents, Heidrick and Struggles (1967), a management consulting firm specializing in executive selection, described the typical profile of a president. According to their findings, presidents must acquire broad administrative skills and also have experience in marketing, planning, or financial management and be able to motivate others. The experiences that contributed most to achievement of a successful career were found to be general administration (29 percent), marketing (21 percent), and finance (15 percent). All other factors were significantly less important as contributors to success as an executive.

Heidrick and Struggles's findings reinforced Copeman's (1974) study of CEOs. The factors that Copeman found to be important in executive success were (1) ability to handle and motivate people (44 percent of executives), (2) analytical skills and creativity (27 percent), (3) personal drive, determination, and status (13 percent), (4) knowledge of the business or trade (9 percent), and (5) other requirements (7 percent). Copeman also found that the majority of chief executives were extroverts and that 49 percent of them had acquired "system" skills by the time they had reached age thirty. Over 76 percent of the executives also had developed confidence in their social skills by that time.

In another study of what contributes to successful management, Morris (1972) found that successful executives employ intuition, have a high tolerance for ambiguity and uncertainty, learn from past decisions, are willing to seek aid, are sensitive to stress, are keenly perceptive and aware of goals, and are able to think abstractly and consider the consequences of their decisions. These attributes match almost precisely the analytical/conceptual/directive styles.

Given the difficulty in readily identifying a person's innate qualities, it is small wonder that in their search for senior executives, companies spend considerable time and money to find those individuals who fit the job requirements. For example, NCR Corporation combed through 4,000 company records simply to identify 828 prospects whose performance was rated high. They used psychological tests to determine whether the individuals had the "potential" to gravitate toward the executive position. This long and often tortuous process, while successful in finding qualified individuals, can be time consuming; and, in the process, "good" candidates can be overlooked.

A screening approach is obviously desirable to quickly identify the most likely executive candidates. In case after case, our data show that style patterns are, in fact, correct predictors of the attributes needed for alignment with a given job. The Army Research Institute (Implementation of . . . , 1987) tested fifty-eight brigadier generals with the Decision Style Inventory. The following year, they tested an additional sixty-one brigadier generals. The objective of the study was to determine whether it would be possible to enhance leadership capabilities. The Army Research Institute has used the Decision Style Inventory as part of its Leadership Enhancement Program and is now evaluating the results.

9

●II●II●II●II●II●II●II●II●II●II●II●II●II●II●II●II●II●II●II●II●II●II●II●II●II●II●II●II●II●II●II●

Psychological Antecedents
of Decision Style

The watershed theorist of style is Carl Jung. His theory of psychological types (Jung, 1923) was the first comprehensive theory of style. Everything that came before it seems to have been leading up to his ideas. Indeed, as an ardent student of mythology and history, Jung drew extensively on a broad range of early philosophical and psychological writings as well as on his own extensive clinical practice. Everything that comes after Jung seems to presuppose his findings, even if, as is the case with the initial development of the DSI, it did not explicitly draw on them.

There are substantial conceptual and empirical correlations between Jung's psychological types and the notions of style embodied in our formulation of style. Before we explore these relationships, however, we will first establish Jung's place in the history of style. To do this, we will begin by explaining his theory in managerial terms. We will then review some of the important philosophical developments that influenced his thinking and discuss the work of several of his contemporaries and followers. Finally, we will explore how this foundation of research and thinking has led to the modern concepts of managerial decision styles. We believe that this review will help the reader to understand the language of style in the context of the wealth of knowledge that others have contributed.

Jung's Theory of Psychological Style

After years of reflection and work with patients, Jung published his theory of psychological types. He concluded that there are two fundamental ways in which people react psychologically to the situations with which they are faced. The characteristic tendencies to respond to a situation in a constant and predictable way he called "preferences," which determine how people carry out two types of psychological functions. The "perceiving" function involves one's preferences as to how one acquires information about a situation. The second function involves three stages. It is determined by one's preferences for the means of internalizing information, processing it, and finally making judgments about it. This he called the "judging" function.

These two precepts were then further subdivided. The acquisition of information through the perceiving function can take one of two forms, depending on the flow of events and how stimuli reach a person's mind. One way of receiving information about a situation is from external sources, using the five senses. That is, we see it, hear it, smell it, taste it, or feel it. This is the "sensing" function. The other way to receive information is to extract it from the recesses of our minds. Such information is commonly called ideas "out of the blue"; even in more respectable discussions, such words as *insights, hunches, premonitions,* and even *telepathic messages* have been used. This internal source of information—the "sixth sense," as it is sometimes called—Jung referred to as the "intuiting" function.

Having acquired information by means of the sensing and/or intuiting function, the mind is now ready to evaluate it. Again, as with the perceiving function, Jung subdivided the judging function into two subfunctions, depending on the type of evaluation used. One approach is to take the information given, break it up into its component parts, compare and contrast them, and then determine how they are related to one another. This use of logic and analysis in an impersonal process he called the "thinking" function. In contrast, however, information can be evaluated holistically, without thinking about it in terms of individual chunks. One's "gut reaction" may be that the collection of information currently being experienced is good or bad, pleasing or distasteful, beautiful or ugly, or exciting or dull. These evaluations emanate not from our rational considerations of the information given but from our emotional responses to it. This spontaneous response to a situation derives from the "feeling" function. One may make feeling judgments without necessarily being aware of them or how they were arrived at. Thinking judgments, on the other hand, are made consciously, and the steps leading up to them are retraceable.

It bears repeating that each of us possesses some aspects of each of these functions and of necessity uses them every day. As Jung summarizes, "These four functional types correspond to the obvious means by which consciousness obtains its orientation to experience. *Sensation* (i.e. sense perception) tells you something exists; *thinking* tells you what it is; *feeling* tells you whether it is agreeable or not; and *intuition* tells you whence it comes and where it is going" (Jung, 1971, p. 61). What differs among people—and this is the essence of one's style—is the relative emphasis that each person places on each of these functions. By relating the two perceiving functions to the two judging functions, Jung constructed a fourfold theory of psychological style. This theory and its relationship to the DSI are summarized in Figure 7.

Figure 7. Jung's Typology Applied to DSI Styles.

		Thinking (*T*)	Feeling (*F*)
Perception functions (How information is acquired)	Intuiting (*N*)	*NT* Type (Analytical)	*NF* Type (Conceptual)
	Sensing (*S*)	*ST* Type (Directive)	*SF* Type (Behavioral)

Thinking (*T*)   Feeling (*F*)

Judgment functions
(How information
is evaluated)

The styles that we have described as directive, analytical, behavioral, and conceptual can also be classified according to Jung's typology as *ST* (sensing/thinking), *NT* (intuiting/thinking), *SF* (sensing/feeling), and *NF* (intuiting/feeling), respectively. Harold Geneen is an example of a directive who can also be described as an *ST* in Jung's typology. He emphasized his sensing and thinking functions as he collected reams of data, filed them into his attaché cases, and studied them in order to keep control at ITT. Robert McNamara emphasized his thinking and intuitive functions as he analyzed situations at the Pentagon and sought to discover the most logical frameworks for analyzing and solving problems of defense and national security. Alfred Marrow stressed his feeling and intuiting functions when he empathized with the plight of his workers and sought new organizational structures that would help them each live more productive and rewarding lives. Edwin Land accentuated his intuitive and thinking functions as he conceived of a new camera that would produce pictures almost instantaneously.

This conceptual association between decision style and Jung's theory has been established empirically by means of correlations with the Myers-Briggs Type Indicator—an instrument developed by followers of Jung to categorize people into his types. The utility of having established this association is that it makes available to users of the DSI the wealth of findings from research that has been conducted in the Jungian tradition, including insights from some of the sources that Jung himself used.

Historical Background

During most of human civilization, philosophers have argued, on the basis of their theories of the universe at large, that there are fundamentally two mental styles. The first, similar to our directive style, focuses on the concrete and the here and now—that is, facts and things rational and observable. The other, which is similar to our conceptual style, focuses on the abstract and atemporal—that is, ideas and things coming from the heart. The two are in opposition to one another but are also necessary for each other. A person's mind oscillates back and forth between these two somewhat pure states, although it might linger in one state longer than in the other. When it does, that is its preferred state.

The earliest recorded development of this idea of two types is in the *I-Ching*, the Chinese "Book of Changes" (Wilhelm, 1967), which is considered to epitomize the wisdom of ancient China. In about 500 B.C., Confucius and his disciples carried a leather thong–bound copy of the book with them while in exile from the kingdom of Lu. During periods of rest, they would read from its pages and contemplate its meaning. The *I-Ching* is based on the permutations around two basic symbols. The

Ch'ien   K'un

left hexagram, Ch'ien, which represents the yang, is the ancient root of the directive. It is the extreme masculine power of the cosmos and is characterized by daylight, heat, dryness, mountains, and rock—all things that can be sensed—as well as force, penetration, and movement—all concepts that pertain to practical and purposeful activity.

K'un, the counterpart, represents the yin, the root of the conceptual. Its broken line represents the dark, yielding, receptive primal source characterized as female, the flowing stream, a valley, absorption, and rest—all things that are more mysterious and operate at the "meta-level." The text describes it as a state of "receptive devotion. Thus the superior man who has breath of character carries the outer world." One recent student of the text links K'un with the heart in the Bible and consequently with the subconscious mind.

These ancient symbols had considerable influence on Carl Jung as he struggled to develop his theory of psychological types. Their importance to him was recounted in the foreword that he wrote to his friend Richard Wilhelm's (1967) popular translation of the *I-Ching*. In the yang, he saw the thinking and sensing functions at work. In the yin, he saw the intuiting and feeling functions at work. Most impressive, however, were the dynamics between the two. The yin and the yang in Taoist and other early writings were conceived of as being two great polar opposite but complementary forces that combined to produce all that comes into being. Jung speculated that this is also how the mind works. This is a powerful insight. As we will see, every theory and application of style makes a distinction between emphasis on the concrete and objective, on the one hand, and on the abstract and subjective, on the other. Moreover, every theory also stresses the need for both forces to work together in harmony if either one is to be successful. For the individual, this means obtaining a balanced psyche and alignment in his or her work. For an organization, it means forming good "marriages" among styles—such as Honda and Fujisawa had. This involves assigning people to jobs that fit their style and aligning the organization with the demands of its environment.

Eastern philosophy has not had a monopoly on dualistic thinking. Early Western mythology contains it as well. Apollo, the son of Zeus, was rivaled only by his father as the highest god in the Greek pantheon. He was a "man of action," a directive. "He came down furious from the summits of Olympus, bow and quiver upon his shoulder," recites Homer in the *Illiad*, "and the arrows rattled on his back with the rage that trembled within him." As the Greek legends have it, Apollo was not only quick and decisive, but he was also orderly and rational. Nietzsche characterized Apollo as one who had the will to use power.

Nietzsche also uncovered in Greek mythology the counterpart to Apollo's masculine power role, someone more in the mold of the conceptual style—Dionysus, the feeling person, emotional, ecstatic, and, though born a man, the god of fertility and creativity and the personification of feminism. Dionysus was the god of the ancient rituals out of which modern drama emerged. Unlike Apollo, who was remote and unapproachable, Dionysus participated in the festivities and shared in the excitement. Through this concern for humanity and struggles of life, Dionysus became the god of the poor and the oppressed. For a while, he did not figure prominently in the culture or the power structure of ancient Greece (Homer hardly mentions him). Ironically, it was the tyrants of Athens and of Sicyon, all strong characters in the directive style, who returned Dionysus to prominence. Out of avarice and in an attempt to gain popular political support, these leaders started the Great Dionysia at Athens, at which the creative spirit of Dionysus was celebrated in comedies, tragedies, dancing, and singing.

Nietzsche found religious significance in the contrasting world views of Apollo and Dionysus, but there is a practical, psychological significance as well. In a letter to *Science,* the Nobel Prize winner Szent-Gyorgyi (1972) used the characteristics of these Greek gods to distinguish between two types of scientists. An Apollonian scientist was depicted in directive/analytical terms as disinterested, impersonal, and methodical, a pursuer of facts and a user of logic. Dionysian scientists, in contrast, were described in more conceptual and behavioral terms. They take a deep personal involvement in the phenomena that they study and immerse themselves in every aspect of them. From this intense involvement springs a depth of insight and understanding that is qualitatively different from that of the Apollonian. Dionysians are imaginative, speculative, and holistic in their thinking and tend to observe conflict in human affairs. Their logic is dialectical.

The twofold world of the ancients predominated until Jung's comprehensive theory was developed and the importance of the additional dimensions was realized. Jung's concepts, for example, led Mitroff and Kilmann (1978) to propose four archetypes of scientific inquiry, in counterdistinction to Szent-Gyorgyi's Appollonian and Dionysian: a directive scientist, whose style of inquiry is "the outer manifestation of the inner psychological attitude of the *ST*" (p. 32); an analytical scientist, who uses conceptual inquiry and analysis; a conceptual scientist, who, like the *NF,* takes a deep personal interest in his or her subject matter and studies it by means of a dialectical behavioral logic; and a behavioral scientist, whom they refer to as a "particular humanist" and who uses a logic of the unique and singular to study individuals intensely. Management theory and psychological theory also drew heavily on the richer model of Jung. But this did not happen until well into the twentieth century and after Sigmund Freud and others had paved the way.

More Recent Developments

Eastern philosophy, with its concepts of yin and yang, and early Greek mythology, with its archetypes Apollo and Dionysus, show that, from the beginning of recorded history, thinkers have observed the differences between people, both in the way they react to situations and the way they interact with others. Yet they lacked a coherent theory. Sigmund Freud was to provide this. Though several thinkers discussed the possibility of an unconscious part of the mind during the late eighteenth and the nineteenth centuries, Freud was the first to demonstrate that the unconscious could have effects on conscious processes. The puzzles he sought to solve were how it is that we "know" more than that of which we are consciously aware and how it is that we can act "knowingly" without conscious awareness. These queries led him into deep explorations into the unconscious in search of the primal instincts and drives of human beings. There he found such pathologies as selective forgetting, "Freudian slips" of the tongue, phobias, and anxieties. His most important contribution, however, was establishing the fact that there are unconscious forces that influence the way we think and behave. Furthermore, there are consistencies in these effects. These findings alerted Western society to notions of personality differences.

Soon a Freudian model emerged. The mind was seen as operating at three levels: the cognitive, which involved perceptual and intellectual activities; the emotional; and the conative, which was the seat of instincts and drives. These drives were rather stable but varied from individual to individual in terms of their quality, intensity, and mode of gratification. Individuals also varied with respect to their emotional needs, such as affiliation, harmony, and avoidance of punishment. In this model, instincts and drives emerged from an unconscious "id," moral obligations derive from a preconscious "super ego," and all of these demands are managed by a relatively conscious "ego," which when it gets in trouble protects itself by means of "defense mechanisms." This analytical, though rather mechanistic, model took the concept of decision style well beyond the objective distinctions of the ancients, but it was still a long way from being a useful model for managerial purposes.

Jung met Freud in 1907 and for a little over five years was an ardent disciple and intense collaborator. Due perhaps to his religious upbringing, however, he was a more holistic and organic thinker than Freud. Late in their association, these differences in approach intensified, and in 1913 Jung broke with Freud. Among his reasons for parting was his need to develop his own theory of psychological types. In his practice, Jung had observed two distinctly different attitudes among people: extroversion and introversion. Both of these attitudes were driven by the unconscious. He found amazing consistency as to whether people tended to psychologically orient themselves toward the external world or toward the internal world of their minds. As he delved deeper, additional patterns emerged, and he discovered that these attitudes were systematically carried out by the four functions discussed earlier—sensing, intuiting, feeling, and thinking. Furthermore, there was a consistent pattern of selectivity among these functions. Although every individual possessed all functions, each tended to stress one of the perception functions—either sensing or intuiting—and one of the judgment functions—either thinking or feeling—to the exclusion of the other. The relatively unused functions were relegated to a position of inferiority and became shadow functions. This is the fundamental insight underlying the concept of decision style.

In arriving at his typology, Jung was undoubtedly influenced by the work of Alfred Binet, who is best known as the inventor of intelligence quotient (IQ) tests. Binet was also an avid observer of human behavior. His observations began at home with his two daughters, Marguerite and Armande. Binet saw two clearly different styles, reminiscent of the ancient dichotomies, in his daughters. Marguerite he called an objectivist. She chose the more concrete words from among those in his various compilations, and in his prototype word association tests, she used words related to more contemporary, definable objects. Armande, on the other hand, was a subjectivist. She chose the more abstract words in the lists, which for her conjured up wonderful fantasies and timeless memories. What Binet (1984) had discovered in these family experiments was the distinction between what we call the left brain and the right brain, a distinction that repeats itself throughout the history of style. For Jung, Binet's discovery formed the outermost edges of a psychological space running from the *ST*/objectivist on one end and the *NF*/subjectivist on the other.

During the early part of the twentieth century, a variety of researchers—Binet, Janet, Bleuler, Kretschmer, and Rorschak, to name a few—discovered individual attributes relating to psychological types. None, however, developed a comprehensive theory to rival Jung's. In fact, it was over twenty years after the original publication in 1921 of Jung's *Psychological Types* (Jung, 1923) (the same year that Freud published *Group Psychology* and *Ego Analysis* [Freud, (1921) 1967]) before the next major breakthrough pertinent to our concept of decision styles occurred, and it was initiated by events leading up to the Second World War. The question posed by concerned psychologists in the early 1940s was why so many people had consciously chosen fascism. It was psychologically a very different question from that asked by Freud or Jung. Those explorers had sought to describe the extent of the human mind and the factors affecting it and had, in the process, discovered the unconscious—emotions and drives. These new psychologists, however, focused on the substance of the things that people were consciously aware of and on the mental processes by which they gained their knowledge. They observed, for example, in Italy and then in Germany, the rise of fascism, and they wondered why people seemed to consciously, rather than instinctively, choose a rigid, single-focus, antidemocratic system of government.

T. W. Adorno was among the first to pursue this new direction. Together with Else Frankel-Brunswik, Daniel J. Levinson, and R. Nevitt Sanford, he began a series of studies during the early 1940s that culminated in 1950 with the publication of *The*

Authoritarian Personality (Adorno, Frankel-Brunswik, Levinson, and Sanford, 1950). By analyzing questionnaires administered to hundreds of people in various settings, ranging from family and intimate relationships through managerial situations to national political systems, they uncovered two distinct patterns. One was a flexible pattern, characterized by humanistic, affectionate, egalitarian, and permissive relationships and also, in terms of the DSI, a high tolerance for ambiguity. People with this style invariably chose democracy. The other style—the "authoritarian personality"—was rigid, dogmatic, power oriented, and hierarchical. It tended toward fascism.

Adorno's conclusions provided a basis for a better understanding of our approach to decision styles. He found that "the political, economic, and social convictions of an individual often form a broad and coherent pattern, as if bound together by a 'mentality' or 'spirit,' and that this is an expression of deep lying trends in his personality" (p. 1). As one's personality emerges, the unconscious process teams up with the cognitive, conscious, and ego processes and forms a particular and enduring pattern of thinking, feeling, and behaving. Such characteristic patterns make the individual unique. Personality, then, is *not* behavior—it is what lies behind it—and it is not simply how we respond to situations—it is the "predisposition" to respond to each situation in a specific way. This predisposition derives from one's level of cognitive complexity. People with a need for structure form authoritarian personalities, like those of our directives. People with a high tolerance for ambiguity form more flexible personalities, like those of our conceptuals. These findings form an important part of the language of style and underlie the development of the DSI.

Adorno and his colleagues' work was extended by Milton Rokeach. Rokeach more clearly than his predecessors drew the distinction between the content of one's beliefs and the psychological processes one uses in believing: "it is not so much *what* you believe that counts, but *how* you believe" (Rokeach, 1960, p. 6). In the *Open and Closed Mind,* a new instrument was developed, the Dogmatism Scale, which proved to be remarkably effective in distinguishing between people with open minds and those with closed minds. For example, people with closed minds are, like our analyticals and directives, comparatively focused and analytical, whereas those with open minds are, like our conceptuals and behaviorals, better able to synthesize. Rokeach's distinctions between the characteristics of open and closed minds, similar to those made by the DSI, are shown below:

1. The ability to remember all of the items to be integrated. Open-minded synthesis occurs when "memory is bypassed by seeing to it that the parts are all in the visual field" (p. 287). This synthesis is characteristic of people who score highly on the right brain dimension.
2. The extent to which one is willing to "play along" and to consider more than one possible system or alternative. Willingness to do this is characteristic of people who score highly on our upper half, or idea, orientation.
3. The ability to relate facts about a new situation to past experience. "The less a system was new, the more will synthesis be facilitated; conversely, the newer a system, the more will synthesis be blocked" (p. 287). Such an ability is characteristic of the right brain style.
4. The extent to which the beliefs of a new system are presented piecemeal or all at once. "In those with relatively closed systems, problem-solving is clearly facilitated when parts of the new system are presented all at once 'on a silver platter'" (p. 287). The need for structured observation is indicative of our directive and behavioral styles.
5. The degree of isolation of beliefs within the system. Closed minds have difficulty tolerating ambiguity and bearing with contradictions, as with those whose scores fall on the lower half of the DSI.
6. The approach to ambiguity. Many situations are inherently ambiguous. The closed mind deals with them by breaking them into small parts and attending to each separately, as do people in the left brain category.

These findings suggest, as we have found, that the directive style will be more closed-minded and the conceptual style more open-minded. Adorno's discovery of the role of cognitive complexity in personal decision making and Rokeach's discovery of the role of open- and closed-mindedness in problem solving clearly point to one of the key underlying assumptions of the DSI: the crucial aspects of one's decision making and problem solving are attributable more to personality and cognitive style than to intellectual ability. Their work also demonstrated that reliable instruments can be constructed that can be used to classify people according to their style.

As Adorno and Rokeach were developing quantitative and analytical approaches to the study of personality, a new intellectual field—social psychology—was also being created. It was much more humanistic and action oriented. Under the captivating influence of Kurt Lewin, two maverick psychologists spearheaded this new movement: Henry Murray (1962), the new explorer of psychological depths, and Gordon Allport (1937), the great scholar of humanism and personality. Both were "personologists" who collected extensive clinical evidence showing that a person's behavior consistently bore a distinctive stamp; that is, his or her style. Among Allport and Murray's students was University of Chicago psychologist M. Brewster Smith, a contemporary of Adorno who directed his attention to social attitudes regarding McCarthyism, Russia, and Communism. His results, obtained by quite different methods, are strikingly similar to those of Adorno and Rokeach. Smith (1969) explored, in depth, people's positions on such political questions as "Are you for or against the Truman Doctrine?" He found a strong pattern of consistency in the stances that they took. The majority of people whom he interviewed were well above average in intelligence and social status, yet most of them showed a lack of capacity for abstract thinking. The political attitudes of people with low cognitive complexity were based on sharp stereotypes, and they revealed numerous non sequiturs in their political thinking. The people who were like our conceptuals were less likely to think in terms of stereotypes and also showed more consistency in their overall thinking.

A comprehensive study by Liam Hudson (1966) yielded surprisingly similar results to those of Binet, Adorno, and

Rokeach and provides further support for our distinction between the directive style and the conceptual style. His subjects were British schoolboys between the ages of fifteen and seventeen. Among them he found two clearly different mental processes. He labeled the two groups *divergers* (these are like our right brain conceptuals) and *convergers* (these are like our left brain directives). Divergers were extremely sensitive people who created their own personal and global descriptions of the situations that they faced. They always enlarged the problems that they were given, expanded the boundaries of consideration, and sought new things to consider and then composed stories to describe and explain the new visions that they had created. In short, divergers were holistic in their approach. In contrast, the more directivelike convergers were narrow and focused in their point of view.

While the divergers dreamed, the convergers concentrated on practical results. Convergers gathered large amounts of impersonal facts about the situations that they faced. Having framed a problem within secure mental bounds, they tended to break it down into a set of relatively independent component parts. That is, Hudson's convergers were reductionistic and analytical in their approach. They also tended to be impatient. Hudson found that some of the extreme convergers that he observed had such a low tolerance for ambiguity—like extreme directives—that they took obviously ill-structured situations and imposed structures on them so that they could indeed "converge" on a single best solution. The convergers' talent for defining things well, gathering and analyzing specific facts, and taking quick and decisive action stood them in good stead when it came to taking examinations. They performed exceptionally well in structured situations, such as taking standardized tests, and they excelled at finding the one single answer to a given question. Divergers, on the other hand, generally did not do as well on such tests. They saw complex possibilities and a diversity of alternative interpretations in each situation, so that, while they did poorly on structured tests, they excelled in highly ambiguous situations that called for creative responses.

Because of a more developed feeling function, divergers displayed their emotions more readily than did convergers. This characteristic was revealed with exceptional clarity in one of the tasks that Hudson asked his subjects to perform. He showed them a set of common, everyday objects, such as a brick, a blanket, a paper clip, and a barrel. Then he asked them the simple question, "How many different uses can you think of for each of these objects?" Divergers consistently created more uses for each object than did convergers. Their uses also differed in quality. Convergers tended to produce more productive and practical uses. A tally of the twenty-five most frequently cited productive uses showed that the first eight on the list were generated exclusively by convergers. At the extremes, some convergers produced potentially practical uses that Hudson described as "morbid and bizarre." For example, "A brick is used to smash one's sister's head in" and "A barrel is used to stuff headless bodies in." "In caricature," Hudson concluded, "the converger takes refuge from people in things; the diverger takes refuge from things in people" (Hudson, 1966, p. 91).

There are two other aspects of Hudson's study that are relevant to the language of style. One is that he found that the distinction between a predisposition toward divergence and a predisposition toward convergence was not clear-cut. Rather, individuals fell along a "spectrum." "Working from one end of the distribution to the other, we find extreme divergers (10 percent); moderate divergers (20 percent); all-rounders (40 percent); moderate convergers (20 percent); and extreme convergers (10 percent)" (p. 41). Why would Hudson observe this nearly bell-shaped distribution? We believe that he did not take into consideration such factors as cognitive complexity and external orientation, which are part of decision styles. Across the spectrum from the style of an extreme converger (directive style in the DSI) to that of an extreme diverger (conceptual style), the mental processes involve increasingly more intuition and feeling and increasingly less emphasis on sensing and thinking. Thus, the existence of analytical and behavioral styles accounts for his observing a large number of "all rounders" and "moderates." In our studies, we found that, in addition to one or more dominant styles, people also have backup or supporting styles. This also accounts for why people fall between the extremes of continuum scales such as Hudson's.

Another significant aspect of Hudson's work is that he tracked the careers of his subjects. Convergers, he discovered, tended to follow careers such as accounting, experimental science, building construction, surgery, and law—all careers in which their structured problem-solving skills could be used. These are the very careers that directives and analyticals tend to gravitate to. Divergers, on the other hand, became artists, teachers, preachers, and creative researchers—conceptual and behavioral type careers in which humanistic and intuitive skills are important. Thus, Hudson found, as we have, that a person with a given style tends to seek out a career that fits that style in search of positive alignment.

Hemispheric Specialization in the Brain

The distinctions made by Jung, Binet, Adorno, Rokeach, and Hudson have found psychological grounding in the findings of hemispheric specialization in the brain. These studies find the left side of the brain to be the primary seat of logical and analytical thinking, while the right side is the primary source of creativity and esthetics. People who score high on the left side of the DSI reveal a strong preference for analytical thinking, which uses the left hemisphere of the brain, whereas those who score high on the right side reveal a preference for holistic thinking, which uses the right hemisphere.

These tendencies were first suggested by researchers who were studying people's eye movements. Among them was Paul Bakan (1971), a psychologist at Simon Fraser University. A group of students who were enrolled in a variety of different schools at the university were observed as they responded orally to a series of questions, and their lateral eye movements were recorded. Previous research had established that there is a general correlation between one's lateral eye movements and the hemisphere of the brain that is being employed—that left eye movements correlate with usage of the right hemisphere of the brain, right eye movements with utilization of the left hemisphere. So, by observing eye movement, Bakan was able to infer which side of the brain the student was using. Students majoring in literature and in the humanities tended predominantly to use the right hemisphere, while students majoring in science and engineering tended to rely on the left hemisphere. A pattern of correlation is found here. The left, or logical, hemisphere is the location of analytical reasoning in the brain. People who use it predominantly gravitate toward careers in science and engineering. And these are the very careers chosen by Hudson's convergers, Jung's high-thinking-function types, and the DSI directives and analyticals, for the same underlying reasons. Similarly, people who stress use of the right, or spatial/relational, hemisphere choose careers in literature and the humanities, just as do conceptuals and behaviorals, divergers, and those who favor the feeling function.

A number of researchers have followed up on Bakan's work, asking a wider variety of questions and tracing the attendant shifts in eye movement. Questions involving logic problems, arithmetic, definitions, and spelling activated the left brain. The right brain was stimulated by questions involving music, spatial relationships, and visualization. In one study, questions were asked concerning whether hate or anger was the stronger emotion. When asked these kinds of questions, the respondents' eyes shot to the left, suggesting that the right hemisphere was actively engaged. Every question calling for an evaluation of emotions yielded the same results, indicating that the right hemisphere is the processor of emotional information and the repository of the feeling function.

Other research on hemispheric specialization of the brain has resulted in additional findings that relate to the language of style and the DSI. Take, for example, the simple problem of remembering faces. Our studies show that to the question on the DSI asking people what they are good at remembering, those classified as conceptuals respond most frequently with the choice "people's faces." This would suggest that recognizing people's faces is a function carried out in the right hemisphere of the brain. Psychological studies on facial agnosia—the inability of a person to recognize familiar faces—have reached the very same conclusion. Facial agnosia is most frequently observed in patients with lesions or other damage in the right hemisphere of the brain. When these occur, these individuals simply forget other people's faces because they cannot visualize them adequately. Thus, there is a correlation between remembering faces, which people with the conceptual style do well, and the functioning of the right hemisphere of the brain.

Although hemispheric specialization has been recognized for over 150 years—a French country doctor, Marc Dax (Springer and Deutsch, 1981), delivered the first paper describing it in 1836—there is still much to learn. Research on the functioning of the left versus the right side of the brain is still continuing. Ethical considerations, however, restrict the amount of controlled research that can be undertaken. Furthermore, some inconsistencies are found in the results reported. Still inconclusive, for example, are such issues as what kinds of information are communicated from one side to the other, whether each hemisphere can operate independently, whether one hemisphere can learn to function like the other, and whether the primary functioning of each hemisphere is innate or is learned. Despite the many unknowns, there are relationships that we find compelling with regard to our theory of decision styles. In general, the two hemispheres of the brain relate to two different cognitive styles: the left side to the directive/analytical style and the right side to the conceptual/behavioral style. Also, the characteristics describing these styles correspond with what is known of left and right brain functions.

The Myers-Briggs Type Indicator

There is one final development in the Jungian tradition that has an important bearing on the DSI. In 1957, the *Myers-Briggs Type Indicator* (MBTI) was published (Briggs and Myers, 1957). This is the first reliable instrument that effectively sorts people into Jungian categories: introverted/extroverted, sensing/intuiting, thinking/feeling, and perceiving/judging. By asking a large number of questions about one's personal life, the MBTI has been used to classify people according to Jung's psychological types and to show their inclination to pursue certain careers. The MBTI has proved to be extremely useful for research purposes and has been used extensively in vocational and personal counseling to aid in job placement. It has disadvantages for managerial use, however. The questions are very personal, and therefore many managers find them irrelevant or, at worst, an invasion of privacy. Also, the full questionnaire is long and time consuming to administer. Finally, the instrument classifies people as single types, with no reference to multiple dominance or to backup styles. Nevertheless, the Myers-Briggs Type Indicator has made a major contribution to the measurement of styles. It has resulted in a substantial collection of data and research on Jungian styles and career preferences.

The MBTI over the years has served as the empirical anchor for classifying people according to style and has been repeatedly tested as to its validity and reliability. It consists of 166 well-designed items with apparent construct validity, and the overall patterns of scores obtained tend to correlate highly with such important characteristics as esthetic and vocational preferences, aptitudes, needs, creativity, academic achievement, and work habits (Coan, 1978). Reliability data are available in the MBTI manual (Myers, 1976, p. 20). Review articles show that there is a high degree of internal consistency among responses to related questions and that repeated applications of the instrument to the same person yield the same results. On the rare occasions in which differences are found in these test-retest studies, the differences usually result from changes in just one preference, and that is usually the one that is the least preferred style (McCaulley, 1981). The MBTI has also been shown to perform relatively well in predicting a college student's choice of a major and success in a collegiate program (Stricker and Ross, 1964). Two deficiencies have been uncovered in the MBTI. The scales are not truly bipolar, orthogonal, or independent, and the judging/perceiving dimension departs from Jung's original construct, hampering its theoretical validity.

Because the MBTI has been such a successful instrument for assessing style, we felt that it was important that the DSI be compared to it. Studies by Dickel (1983), Mann (1982), and Craft (1984) all show a highly significant relationship between the two test instruments; that is, they are conceptually and empirically consistent. In these cross-validation studies, the following patterns emerge: the directive style most resembles the Jungian *ST* type as measured by the MBTI and is least like the *NT* type. The analytical style most resembles the *NT* type, somewhat resembles the *ST* type, and is least like the *SF*. The conceptual style is most similar to the *NF* type, is somewhat similar to the *NT*, and is least like the *ST*. The behavioral style most resembles the *SF* type and is least like the *NT*. Karl Dickel (1983) found further relationships between the two instruments. People scoring high on the lower-half styles on the DSI tend to be classified as more extroverted by the MBTI, whereas upper-half styles are classified as more introverted. The conceptual style favors the perceiving functions (sensing and intuiting), whereas the analytical and behavioral styles favor the judging functions. Dickel interpreted these findings in terms of McKenney and Keen's (1973) distinction between a ''receptive'' mind and a ''perceptive'' mind. Conceptuals are receptive and are open to new events as they develop, whereas analyticals and behaviorals are more perceptive in that they consider new information only within the context of a preconceived framework. For analyticals, these a priori frameworks are based on logic and analysis; for behaviorals, they are based on emotions and previous experience.

There is a powerful conclusion to be drawn from these twentieth-century developments as they pertain to the DSI. Freud established the existence of the unconscious and its role in influencing a person's behavior. Jung gave us a well-developed theory of personality types and styles. Binet, Hudson, and others provided substantial clinical and empirical evidence that supported Freud's and Jung's insights. Adorno and Rokeach demonstrated that one's psychological type strongly influences the stance that one takes on many issues. The notion that one's style has a high degree of permanency is suggested by the fact that it correlates with the side of the brain that is activated. Finally,

Adorno, Rokeach, and Myers and Briggs proved that reliable instruments can be developed to measure one's style and personality; in particular, the MBTI adequately measures Jung's psychological types. The DSI, with fewer and more managerially oriented questions, also measures style on the basis of its own theory, and it also correlates highly and consistently with Jung's concepts as measured by the MBTI. The DSI is a valid test instrument that is fully consistent with twentieth-century psychological research. In the next chapter, we will show its relationship to managerial research and applications.

10

Development of Decision Style
and Situation Alignment

From its very start perhaps some 30,000 years ago in the underground caves of France and Spain, civilization was characterized by people who used their minds to align themselves with their environments so as to better cope with nature's forces. Cro-Magnon people, as an illustration, were primarily hunters and gatherers. Their work environment was the great valleys of the Pyrenees, in which herds of horses, wild oxen, reindeer, ibexes, and bison roamed. We know that as Ice Age glaciers receded to the north, the herds followed behind, seeking the newly awakening foliage and the lush grasses. In the process, the once concentrated herds spread out into the meadows and valleys and became more sparse. This presented a problem for the hunters, because now the search for meat took them many miles further away from their cave sanctuaries. Artists and anthropologists believe that the pressures for survival brought about by the long hunting treks and the need to find meat gave rise to the marvelous cave paintings and engravings found in Lascaux and Altamira.

The paintings also served an important instructional purpose. Each new generation had to learn about their quarry and methods for hunting them. The pictures etched into the cave walls were the media for imparting this education. The paintings were art used as the means for obtaining meat. These people developed rituals and ceremonies to dramatize them and served to bring social cohesion to the tribe. In the process, the mind was activated and expanded, driven by the need to understand the paintings and the message that they carried about survival. These primitive minds, however, were not as fully developed as the modern mind. In this primitive environment, the dominant needs were what Maslow (1954) called "physiological needs"—those that are at the bottom of the hierarchy of personal needs. While decision styles must have emerged among these peoples, they would have been quite different from styles of the modern, more developed mind. Decision style as we know it today responds to a diverse environment, based on exposure to knowledge, education, and interpersonal interaction.

Nevertheless, we see that, even in this simple society, the four environmental forces that we identified in Chapter Four were at work, serving as pressures that people had to respond to. The work environment encompassed the range in which the herds grazed. The task was arduous and required hunting over long distances. The tribe or clan of a Cro-Magnon engendered forces in the social and organizational realm that dealt with land, totems, customs, and, of course, the cave paintings. These forces served to bind the people together into a community with privileges and obligations. Because so much of a person's life was devoted to securing food and survival, the dominant needs were physiological.

Given these harsh and confining conditions, it is highly likely that only a limited capacity for decision styles emerged and that a rather homogeneous cognitive orientation existed. And yet, as the cave art bears witness, even with these limitations, some of what we now call the conceptual style was present in these primitive peoples. They were able to conceive the idea of painting animals on walls and to develop technology using charcoal, stick brushes, and paint made from powdered earth colors mixed with animal fat. The creative process of the conceptual was also responsible for the symbolism and rituals that evolved around the paintings. Those who originated these ideas must have been psychologically distinct from, for example, the more directive individuals who led the tribespeople on the hunt or the behaviorals who provided warmth and comfort in the caves. Even in this most simple of societies, those who had a distinctive style, conscribed though it may have been, had to find effective alignment in order to succeed with their personalities.

We can only conjecture about the behavior and psychological life of people who lived long ago. The traces of evidence that survive from the Paleolithic era are meager. We do, however, have better evidence about contemporary "primitive" tribes. At least one observer, William Irwin Thompson (1971), has speculated on the character of primitive tribes by considering aspects of the social structure of extant tribes. His conclusions can be interpreted in ways that shed light on decision styles as well.

An interesting perspective is provided in the hunting sequence in John Marshall's film *The Hunters*. Four bushmen set out across the Kalahari Desert in search of food. The land is windblown and arid, and their tools are few, consisting primarily of small arrows tipped with a slow-working poison. A giraffe is spotted and stalked. After several disappointing attempts, an arrow finally hits its target. The story documents the events that unfold as the four hunters trail the injured animal and the lethal poison seeps into its body. It will be more than a week before the poison kills it, and during that time the giraffe will travel far. If they lose track of it, they will fail to bring food back to the tribe.

Challenged by the demands of their task, the four bushmen form a cohesive social structure, and each assumes a special social role. The plan of how they will pursue their prey is developed by the "Headman," who is the source of reason and authority among them. The hunting itself is directed by a strong and graceful man called the "Beautiful," who assumes the role of the "Hunter." As they track the animal through the veldt, they stop at a spring for water. Is it potable? The group turns to the one who plays the role of the "Shaman." He performs a magical ceremony and, having reached some cosmic force, determines that the water is safe. They drink and continue their quest. It is a toilsome undertaking, and to lighten their load, from time to time the fourth member of the party, the "Clown," pokes fun at the ideas of the "Shaman." He serves to remind them that they are human.

The environment of the Kalahari, as it is for all hunting and gathering societies, is harsh. There is little economic surplus available. The minds of the tribesmen are absorbed with the rigors of survival, and so the germinal development of style never progresses much further. The development of cognitive style would require an economic breakthrough. This came much later, in the Middle East.

The Agricultural Revolution

In about 7000 B.C., in a land covering the territory that is modern-day Israel, Syria, Turkey, Iran, and Iraq, two important innovations occurred. People stopped roaming the earth in search of food and instead started raising it. Hunting was replaced by animal husbandry and the domestication of wild herds. Gathering was replaced by cultivation of wheat, barley, and rice. These two innovations changed the character of the four forces that affected individuals. The work environment became a more sedentary year-round settlement in which growing seeds and caring for livestock became the most important task. To the basic physiological needs were added the needs for safety and security. Coincidentally, this became necessary also because the sources of food were stationary and thus more vulnerable. As people came together in fertile areas, they formed social groupings that were more urban, stratified, specialized, and politically organized than those found in primitive tribes. This was possible because the change from food gathering to food producing created an economic surplus that freed people's minds to specialize and to pursue their innate interests more fully. The "Hunter" became the professional soldier and formed an institution (which today we call the military) that served to protect the agriculturally based society. The "Headmen" became the lords and barons. The "Shaman" became the religious leader. And the "Clown" became the artisan or critic. Increased specialization and additional psychic energy released by economic surplus allowed the mind to develop its style. The directive, analytical, conceptual, and behavioral styles began to take form.

Psychological and economic specialization, however, brought about new pressures for alignment. There was a larger range of roles, jobs, and careers to be filled in the new agricultural society and a broader set of cognitive styles to be fitted into them. The problem of matching the right person with the right position became more difficult for individuals and for society as a whole.

The Industrial Revolution

The eighteenth century introduced another great revolution. It was based on innovations that were to change social structures even more radically than had cultivation and husbandry. During this period, mechanical technologies such as the flying shuttle, steam engine, water-powered spinning frame, spinning jenny, locomotive, power loom, and cotton gin were invented. The revolution began in England, where, to take advantage of these new technologies, a new form of social structure was created—the factory. James Wedgewood's pottery factory at Eturia, near Stoke-upon-Trent, which opened in 1769, was among the first of this new form. Only thirty years later, moreover, Eli Whitney built a firearms factory in New Haven, Connecticut, in which mass-production techniques were applied. In these factories, machines and management techniques such as the division of labor were used to produce goods rather than crops. Increasingly, these goods were made out of metal, wood, or minerals, which meant that the ability to acquire these materials would become a source of wealth.

The work environment of the industrial society required many specialized jobs and tasks as well as new skills. Major social changes took place as people moved from rural areas to form cities around the factories so that they might work and earn wages. These movements necessitated new social structures. The advent of the corporation created the need for organizations to administer and manage factories and their related business processes. The new wealth that was created permitted people's immediate concerns to move beyond safety, security, and physical survival to needs for affection, belonging, and love. These latter needs developed in the new social settings and gave rise to additional personal needs for prestige, competency, and power. All of these needs emerged as a consequence of the new economic conditions.

During this industrial era, the range of decision styles expanded once more. As diversity and specialization in society came into being, there were more opportunities for concentrating intently within one's style. The behaviorals became artists and social workers, the conceptuals became planners and creators, the analyticals became scientists and financial analysts, and the directives became accountants, technicians, and supervisors. Securing alignment in this industrial society became more difficult as the different styles sought to avail themselves of the many and more varied opportunities for jobs and roles, especially when we consider style patterns, since individuals generally could not use more than a single style.

Kurt Lewin and Managerial Style

If Carl Jung proved to be the central figure in the conceptual development of the psychological theory of decision styles, Kurt Lewin (1936) must be considered the key contributor to its managerial applications. Jung's psychological theory relates primarily to the mind's internal predisposition to view reality in a given way. As we have seen, however, a useful managerial theory must deal with two additional factors: the external factors that impinge on the individual and the ways in which these forces affect decisions. Lewin provided this linkage by means of a deceptively simple formula that says a manager's behavior (B) is a function of his or her style, which Lewin labeled O for "organismic traits," and of the decision or environmental situation (E) in which he or she must take action. His formula for describing expected behavior was $B = f(O,E)$. As can be seen, both style and external conditions must be taken into account to achieve alignment. Relying on this premise, Lewin developed the field force model that was previously described. This approach to understanding behavior he coupled with a new concept of the mind's internal workings, which he called the psychological "life space."

Lewin's notion of a life space added a dynamic dimension to the workings of an individual's mind. In effect, he argued that a person's mind is composed of a series of organic chambers, which are formed and reformed on the basis of experience and predispositions. The force field that a person is in activates a particular mental chamber. The effectiveness of this activated chamber determines the person's effectiveness in dealing with impinging external forces. It also determines the fit between a person and his or her environment. Lewin thus introduced the concept that we call alignment.

Lewin was not an armchair theorist. He and his followers applied these concepts in a wide variety of organizational contexts and evolved a new kind of research, which he called "action research." This approach allowed them to collect research data by working directly with people in organizations and observing the results of their interventions. Alfred Marrow's organization was among the first of many in which this approach was used. The lasting effect of these action-research engagements was that they clearly demonstrated to managers the practical utility of the concepts of environment, style, and fit. These are bedrock concepts in our theory of decision style. They are also essential for practical managerial applications.

The Analytical Approach

Although Jung and Lewin's work was available by the end of the Second World War, managers were slow to adopt their theories in full. At that time, management's attention was largely captivated by the development of computers and the remarkable record achieved by the use of operations research techniques during the war. As they reviewed the evolution of their craft during the industrial era, it became apparent to many managers that their practice had been too ad hoc and overreliant on tradition, and the focus of management education turned to the analytical concepts of mathematics and operations research. As a consequence, the analytical, or heavily left-hemispheric minds, became the ones that were prized. The reigning assumption of the day was that most management problems could be solved by attacking them with well-trained analytical minds using the scientific method. As with all other simplified assumptions, this proved to be inadequate, for reasons directly related to decision styles.

Disillusionment with the analytical approach set in early when many practicing managers failed to implement the solutions provided by their operations research and management science colleagues. What accounted for this? In an attempt to answer this question, management researchers at the University of California, Berkeley conducted a series of experiments in which operations research solutions were provided to subjects in a variety of different situations (Churchman, Ratoosh, and Huysmans, personal communication, 1967). In most of the experimentation, rather involved mathematical models simulated typical business decision making, and the problem presented had a known optimal solution. The participants were divided into several different groups, and stooges were placed in all but one group. In one of the groups, the stooge introduced the optimal answer to the decision problem at hand in the form of a mathematical proof. In another, the stooge presented the answer in terms of a broad verbal discussion emphasizing the principles involved. A control group was also used, in which no stooge was present and no solution was offered. Ironically, the control group generally outperformed the others in making simulated profits. Groups receiving verbal reports, which of necessity were less complete and precise than mathematical reports, came in second. Bringing up the rear were the groups receiving the full (and correct) mathematical solution. With full and complete knowledge for solving the business problem, they still made the least profit.

Among the explanations offered by the researchers for these results was that the subjects had different decision styles. In particular, they argued, most subjects and most managers were not inherently analytical. Consequently, the participants in the study rejected or ignored the mathematical reports, because they did not fit their style. In an impressive study in this series, Huysmans (1970) probed more deeply into the reasons decision makers would reject perfect information. He constructed a test that effectively classified people as either analytical problem-solving types (similar to our left brain style) or heuristic types (similar to our right brain style). The experiment was conducted with a group of subjects using a statistical design in which either a mathematical or a verbal solution was given to subsets of each style type. His results have important implications for the assumptions that executives make about managers' and employees' decision styles. They also speak to decisions about the methods used for providing information to managers.

Not surprisingly, he found that people with a left brain style who were provided with the optimal mathematical solution did indeed tend to implement it more readily than the others. Hence, they earned slightly higher profits in the simulation. Right brain style individuals, however, performed miserably when given the mathematical solution. Their profits were far lower than those of any other group. The two other groups, which received the verbal report, performed nearly as well as did the left brain group that received the mathematical report. Furthermore, the overall average profit made by the groups receiving verbal reports significantly exceeded that made by those receiving the optimal mathematical solution.

Although the approach used in these experiments was exploratory, the results clearly showed the existence of different decision styles. They also demonstrated that differences in style affect a manager's decision-making behavior. This demonstrated to operations researchers that their prevailing and comfortable myth of the mathematical manager was not appropriate. It faced them with a new problem, however: should operations research take into account the psychology and decision style of the managers who used their work? This set many students of management to thinking. Among these operations researchers was C. Jackson Grayson, at that time the dean of the Southern Methodist University Cox School of Business, who couched the problem in terms of cultural differences. Drawing on the "two cultures" of C. P. Snow, he argued: "Managers and management scientists are operating as two separate cultures, each with its own goals, languages and methods. Effective cooperation—and even communication—between the two is just about minimal" (Grayson, 1973, p. 41).

This explanation provided some insight into the problem, but it was not totally satisfying. There is much more to the problems among and between managers and staff in organizations than can be accounted for by the rift between science and the humanities. To explore the question, Peter Keen, under the direction of Harvard Business School professor James McKenney, undertook a comprehensive series of studies on the role of cognitive style in managerial decision making. Although neither author referred directly to Lewin or Jung, traces of these psychologists' influences were present in their research. In the Lewinian tradition, they saw a manager as affected by a set of external forces that are "bounded not only by the formal constraints of his job, but also by the more informal traditions and expectations implicit in his role, by his perception of his position, . . . and by events and cues he sees in his environment" (McKenney and Keen, 1973, p. 81). (The external forces that they identified, incidentally, were those identified by the Four Force Model.) These conditions, the authors argue, affect the problem-finding, problem-recognition, and problem-definition aspects of managerial decision making. They reasoned that the manager's problem-solving strategy depended on his or her cognitive style and how it "fit" the problem being faced. They drew on a variety of relevant background sources—concepts from the Harvard Business School concerning general managers, ideas about information systems, and the theories of psychologist Jerome Bruner (Bruner, Goodnow, and Austin, 1956). Sifting through these, McKenney and Keen developed their own model of cognitive style, which in reality proves to be very Jungian.

In the general managerial context, there was high correlation between the McKenney and Keen model's four proclivities for a manager's mental information processing and Jung's four functions of sensing, intuiting, thinking, and feeling. This result, which was predicted by Mason and Mitroff (1973), was also verified by a study of 107 M.B.A. students using the Myers-Briggs Type Indicator (we believe that the result would have been the same if the DSI had been used). In addition to the MBTI, each M.B.A. student in this study was administered a set of twelve standard reference tests involving cognitive factors. The results were surprisingly similar to Huysman's, showing a particularly strong cleavage between the left brain style (McKenney and Keen called it "systematic" thinking) and right brain style (they called it "intuitive" thinking). People with different styles also had different methods of problem solving. Left brain subjects "tended to be very concerned with defining how to solve a problem. They were conscious of their planning and often commented on the fact that there were other alternative ways of answering the problem" (McKenney and Keen, 1973, p. 84). In contrast, right brain subjects "tended to jump in, try something, and see where it led them. They generally showed a pattern of rapid solution testing," periods of incubation, and selective exploration of seemingly fruitful lines of inquiry (p. 84). A follow-up study of 82 of the M.B.A.s showed that the careers that they chose upon graduation were virtually the same as would be predicted by the DSI or MBTI or by Liam Hudson (McKenney and Keen, 1973).

Convergence of Decision Style Theory

We have seen many aspects of the modern theory of decision styles coming together. A variety of instruments and theories all come to the same conclusion: managers do have different styles, and these styles affect the way they conduct their day-to-day managerial activities, such as problem solving and information processing. Moreover, there is mounting evidence that the myth that the analytical manager is the sine qua non is no longer tenable. In past studies, analytical managers did well on some tasks and very poorly on others. Management scientists and planners in many organizations attacked problems one way while responsible line managers addressed them from a different point of view. None of these parties seemed to be either right or wrong, but they were clearly different. There was something more that had to be considered when studying the managerial mind. Henry Mintzberg sought to find the answer.

Mintzberg, a professor of management at McGill University, in Montreal, Canada, conducted intensive studies of high-level executives involved in policy making (Mintzberg, 1973, 1975). He concluded (which by now should not be surprising) that there are two kinds of thinking at work—the logical, linear, and sequential analytical, on the one side, and the simultaneous, holistic, and relational synthesizer on the other—the same distinction found between left brain and right brain people using the DSI. This distinction he related directly to the two hemispheres of the human brain.

In a popular *Harvard Business Review* article entitled "Planning on the Left Side and Managing on the Right" (Mintzberg, 1976), he ventured the following conclusion: "The important policy processes of managing an organization rely to a considerable extent on the faculties identified with the brain's right hemisphere. Effective managers seem to revel in ambiguity; in complex, mysterious systems with relatively little order" (p. 53). The CEOs that he studied communicated by means of discussion and group meetings, they used soft "feeling" data, they enjoyed ambiguity, and they made decisions by means of judgments rather than through analysis. In one study of strategic decision making, only eighteen of eighty-three policy choices were based on a systematic, analytical evaluation of alternatives of options as they affected the achievement of organizational goals. In short, high-level executives act very like our right brain people, especially conceptuals.

Does this mean that people with left brain styles are not needed or will not succeed in the executive ranks? Of course not! As we have seen in the previous chapters, people of all styles are needed in organizations. Mintzberg makes it clear, however, that left brain types, such as financial planners and management scientists, should be given appropriate roles in their organizations. Their task is to ensure that top managers receive good analytical input. On the basis of his findings, Mintzberg also argues that business schools must learn to educate for the right side of the brain as well as the left. Furthermore, managers must have the wisdom to know when to employ left brain skills and when to use right brain skills. These findings help to answer some of the managerial questions raised by the failures in implementing operations research solutions and by the discovery of differences in psychological types. Yet there is more to be uncovered.

The intuitive manager, as described by former *Fortune* writer Roy Rowan (1986b) in his book of the same name, relies on "hunches" as the basis for business initiative. Rowan cites extensive examples from his interviews, which included CEOs such as Mary Kay, Roy Ash, Edgar Bronfman, H. Ross Perot, Donald Rumsfeld, Roger Staubach, Fran Tarkenton, Peter Ueberroth, and Ray Kroc. All followed their intuition and feelings, yet each was able to separate hope from hunch and wishful thinking from intuition. They also seemed to have a special skill for making "the mover and the monitor" work together. The mover uses the creative impulses from the right hemisphere, and the monitor uses the logical, linear functions of the left. To be effective, both must work together as dynamic opposites, in a manner similar to the match of the yin and the yang.

Our studies using the DSI corroborate Rowan's findings. As we related in Chapter Six, many senior executives score high on both the conceptual and directive styles. This combined style we call the "northeast crossover" entrepreneurial types (D + C). These decision makers deal effectively with all phases of problem solving. They seem able to effectively swing from an open, intuitive, feeling mode—the right brain mover—to a closed, thinking, sensing mode—the left brain monitor. Rowan's interviews of leading executives throughout the world and Mintzberg's in-depth studies confirm our experience with the DSI, which shows that the ability to use both right brain conceptual and left brain directive styles is typical among many senior managers.

When faced with a problem, managers will often consider many possibilities, usually with insight and enthusiasm and a great deal of personal involvement, just as Edwin Land did when he invented the Polaroid camera. Then they focus on the facts, the practical implications, and the procedures for getting things done. These shifts continue until the problem is brought to a successful conclusion. The screen writer Ingmar Bergman summed up the essence of this oscillation in styles by recognizing that to both create and produce successful films one has to use both intuition and logic. It is analogous to throwing a spear into the dark and then having to be logical about where to find it.

This pendulum effect has been observed among successful managers in companies such as Procter & Gamble. When recording the activities of a corporate staff group that was engaged in research and development on consumer products, Carlsson, Keane, and Martin (1976) saw clear shifts in the decision styles that project managers used during each phase of a project's life cycle. The project managers began with the broadest situational concerns, such as What business are we in? and What alternatives might we pursue? This is the conceptual, or right brain, in operation. Having thus identified their problem, the managers swung to a more focused directive, or left brain, style. In this new mind set, they concerned themselves with establishing criteria for evaluating alternatives so that they could arrive at a solution. However, once their directive style efforts yielded a viable solution, they changed their style again. Now they used their conceptual style as they searched for the right people to implement the solution and for ideas on how to produce the product and position it in the marketplace. Having arrived at a general strategy for taking the product to market, the managers swung back to the directive style once more. They made focused decisions on product sales objectives, production, and consumer testing programs. Once this was completed, it was time to become conceptual again. New ideas for product strategy were generated, with special care given to understanding the ultimate consumer. Swinging back to the directive style again, specific targets were set and action was taken to implement the consumer testing program. And so it went. These effective managers oscillated back and forth between the conceptual right brain and directive left brain styles until the total problem was solved.

This oscillatory model seems to describe the mental processes of senior managers as well. Harvard Business School professor John P. Kotter (1982b) spent a number of days with each of fifteen senior executives to see how they operated and what made them tick. Two critical activities that he observed overwhelmed all others: developing and maintaining an extensive interpersonal network and formulating and executing an agenda. Each of the activities requires both right and left brain functioning, but the right brain seemed to dominate. As a follow-up on Kotter's findings, Daniel J. Isenberg (1984) sought to pinpoint more accurately and to establish with tighter empirical methods what goes on inside the minds of senior managers. He spent anywhere from one to twenty-five days with each of twenty-five executives, observing them, grilling them, and talking to their colleagues. In particular, he asked them to recount their thoughts as they did their work. The pattern that emerged is familiar. "In making their day-to-day and minute-by-minute tactical maneuvers, senior executives tend to rely on several general thought processes such as: intuition; managing a network of interrelated problems; dealing with ambiguity, inconsistency, novelty, and surprise; and finally integrating action with the process of thinking" (p. 89). The first three are generally right brain processes, whereas the last—integrating action into the process of thinking—is largely left brain. So the oscillation phenomenon was also present with those senior executives.

The swings that Isenberg observed, however, were not as easy to trace as were those experienced by Carlsson, Keane, and Martin's project managers at Procter & Gamble; they took place almost instantaneously. Senior managers "think while doing." Management psychologist Karl Weick (1984) has also observed this phenomenon and has arrived at the same conclusion. These results further support an important aspect of the DSI. In addition to revealing one's dominant, backup, and least preferred styles, the DSI provides a measure of one's flexibility. Because of the DSI's measure of dominance, especially between right and left brain styles, one can determine the ease with which an individual can accommodate more than one style. Other instruments tend to emphasize a single dominant style and thus do not provide input on flexibility.

A comprehensive theory of managerial style, one that deals with different problem-solving types, split brain usage, and flexibility among styles, has led management theorists once again back to Jung and Lewin. Most recent attempts at an integrative approach to management thinking, such as that of professors John Slocum of Southern Methodist University and Don Hellriegel of Texas A & M University (Slocum and

Hellriegel, 1983), draw explicitly on Jung for their model of how the manager's mind works and implicitly on Lewin in their recognition of the importance of the managers' environment, how it affects them, and how they scan it. From our perspective, the combined Four Force Model and four basic styles of the DSI provide the integration and predictive validity that support the search for a more comprehensive theory that helps explain managerial decision making and also helps determine when the manager is aligned with the job and the environment.

Conclusions

A number of conclusions can be drawn from tracing the historical background of the language of style. First, it is clear that people possess different mental propensities, which we call styles, and that these differences lead to differences in behavior and decision making. Second, a number of instruments have been used to measure these differences and to classify people. Third, when the diverse theories, approaches, and observations are reduced to their essence, there is an amazing amount of similarity in the findings. The recurring themes are:

1. The mind acquires information in two ways: through the senses and by intuiting. A person's cognitive complexity influences the preference for how information is acquired and processed mentally.
2. The mind evaluates information through either thinking or feeling. Thinking tends to stress the objective focus and is task oriented, whereas feeling deals with the subjective and is people oriented.
3. There are at least two but generally four style categories. (In the case of the MBTI and the DSI, there are four primary styles, each of which can be divided into four substyles, giving a total of sixteen basic substyles.)
4. The two styles identified by the ancients are conceptually very similar to and correlate with the current distinction between the left and right hemispheres of the brain.
5. There is a high correlation among the various instruments

used to classify people according to style. This supports a consistency in views of people's decision making propensities.

6. These correlations have related the Jungian to the DSI model of style.

7. Each theory of style involves the tasks to be done, interpersonal interaction, and problem solving. Therefore, the decision situation confronting the executive should be taken into account to determine the most effective alignment.

8. Every attempt to incorporate external forces in a theory of style is consistent with Lewin's research and is explainable by the Four Force Model.

9. Successful performance, then, requires alignment between the executive's style and the decision situation that he or she faces.

Fourth, research and experiments involving managers at work or engaged in the problem-solving process uncover the same recurring themes. These studies of executives and managers underscore the need for managers to understand differences in style and to incorporate these in the design of their own and their organizations' activities. However, the culture of an organization tends to define the internal environment, which either facilitates or inhibits effective performance and change. This suggests that executives will require new ways of thinking to deal with the broader aspects of problem solving and the holistic approaches needed to understand organizations. Consequently, right brain styles—the conceptual and behavioral—will become increasingly important in a highly competitive environment. The right brain tends to focus on human needs and to provide openness and support to members of the organization. The right brain manager is able to visualize decision situations more easily than the left brain type where people are an important aspect of the problem and where vision and creativity are important parts of the task. Historically, the left brain function was the one that predicted managerial success. While the need to accomplish results is as real as ever, the ability to work with and through the organization is becoming increasingly important and is shifting the emphasis from the more rigid and autocratic orientation of the left brain to the more open and supportive orientation of the right brain.

The historical evidence and current research all support the notion of these two distinctive styles described by hemispheric specialization. Ongoing research has shown that there are at least four basic styles such as described by the Jungian model or the DSI. Both of these models have shown that there are at least sixteen substyles within the four primary styles. If we add the concept of style "patterns," which accounts for differences in intensity and flexibility, then the DSI can be used to identify up to 256 different patterns. It becomes obvious that, to describe these differences, one needs a language that helps explain behaviors and predict successful career paths. Combining the style of an individual with the environmental forces that influence behavior and decision making, we recognize that the concept of "alignment" is needed to transfer our focus from the "ideal" style to the real world of organizations and the environmental forces that moderate behaviors, affect feelings, and determine viability of responses to situational demands. That our findings are consistent with and supported by the underlying research of Jung in terms of style and Lewin in terms of environmental factors gives us confidence in the research that was used in developing the DSI test instrument and its application to understanding individuals, their roles in organizations, and the criteria for successful alignment of individuals and tasks.

11

●ΙΙ◉ΙΙ◉ΙΙ◉ΙΙ◉ΙΙ◉ΙΙ◉ΙΙ◉ΙΙ◉ΙΙ◉ΙΙ◉ΙΙ◉ΙΙ◉ΙΙ◉ΙΙ◉ΙΙ◉ΙΙ◉ΙΙ◉ΙΙ◉ΙΙ◉ΙΙ◉ΙΙ◉ΙΙ◉ΙΙ◉ΙΙ◉ΙΙ●

Developing Effective
Decision Styles
for a Complex Future

The idea of future conjures up in our minds the uncertainties
and vagaries that confront every manager. What, then, is the
best approach to examining the future of style? We can monitor
technological trends, population growth, or medical progress,
but how do we predict catastrophic events, people's feelings,
or competitors' strategies? The answer may be that, rather than
trying to predict the future, we should determine how best to
cope with its uncertainties. This leads us to the conclusion that
organizations led by executives who can use an adaptive/cop-
ing posture that allows them to accommodate a wide range
of exigencies and who can make the changes needed to meet
new requirements are the ones most likely to be successful in
a highly turbulent environment. We have seen that old-style
management, where decision making, power, and rewards are
concentrated at the top, is clearly failing to achieve exceptional
performance.

   We see case after case where workers are unhappy with
organizational structures that separate thinking from doing and
that deny them autonomy and self-esteem. To be responsive
to external threats and make major moves rapidly and effectively, organizations will have to involve individuals to a greater
extent than is current practice. In his book on *High Involvement
Management,* Lawler (1986) suggests that organizations need

177

to decentralize decision making by trimming the fat and flattening the organizational structure, reward employees for their knowledge and skills so that they can be more effective at responding to new requirements, and tie the employees' economic well-being to the success of the enterprise. These changes would more nearly align employee involvement with concern for performance. High involvement enhances the individual's self-esteem by matching the individual's style with the changing requirements of the work. By maintaining a flexible approach to job-style match, the organization positions itself to more effectively cope with the multitude of forces in the external environment that threaten its survival and effectiveness.

Our perspective of the future started by tracking the evolutionary growth of style, which developed in response to the economic and survival needs of society. We are now confronted with a new set of environmental forces, which will also require a new style of management to cope effectively with these changes.

The Information Age

Today we are in the midst of an important societal change. Our contemporary society is often described as the information age. Information, whether it comes from books, periodicals, television, or computers, dominates the socioeconomic forces that influence our lives. The quest for alignment has become even more difficult as our society has moved into this new age. Information is and has been a necessary component in all societies, but it is only one of four key economic ingredients. The other three are nature, land, and capital (manufactured goods that are used for the production of other goods and services). The role of information today is entirely different from the role that it played in primitive societies. Although there is no question that the cave paintings of Lascaux and Altamira served as vital information to Cro-Magnon society, nature was the dominant force affecting hunting and gathering societies. It dictated their lives and kept them continually on the move. The agricultural revolution required people to put down roots that led to land becoming the dominant economic factor. The advent of machines and more powerful tools shifted the focus once more, this time to capital. And as civilization moved through these eras, the role of information in society continued to assume greater importance.

The transition from an industrial society to an information society has brought about several qualitative changes that affect the environment of all individuals. Emphasis has shifted from transportation, the physical moving of goods and people, to communication, the moving of symbols and ideas among people. Communications today are on a global scale, and messages can traverse any space in a matter of seconds. The standardization of goods and services, made famous by Henry Ford's mass-produced Model T, is giving way to a demand for more variety and customizing as the consumers' vast array of desires is overtaking the producers' limited capacity to provide goods.

The human need for self-determination is affecting social structures as well. The typical hierarchy of authority, with a rigid scalar form of line and staff, is yielding to demands for more active participation on the part of employees and other members of the organization. These trends toward communication, customization, and participation all work together to cause once highly centralized organizations to become more decentralized and dispersed. Now they are woven together by a network of communications links. As these channels become more heavily used, they tend to become clogged. In the process the historical concern about information scarcity is replaced by complaints of information overload.

Turbulent is the word that Fred Emery and Eric Trist used to describe the environment in which we live and manage in the information age. As they saw it, the texture of the causal forces that impinge upon us are numerous, widespread, and unpredictable (Emery and Trist, 1965). Although there is little doubt about the turbulent nature of our environment as part of the information age, societies in this environment can draw on the wealth and surpluses created by previous eras. There are greater opportunities available, but there are also greater threats and ambiguities in this kind of world. In this type of environment, people often aspire to loftier goals, such as self-actualization. It is an inherent human tendency to want self-fulfillment, self-expression, and autonomy from external forces, and these are becoming achievable goals for many.

These changes in the four forces that shape our lives have enormous implications for future decision makers. As the world becomes more complex and more varied, it will demand more intellectual and cognitively oriented participation from people. The range of patterns of style and the intensity with which some people concentrate on their styles will become more relevant to effective performance. In a world with so many different styles, all striving to cope with the turbulent environment, the problem of finding alignment is more difficult than it was in a time when people were often "slotted" for life in one or a few jobs. The language of style increasingly will contribute to executive success, and the DSI will be a helpful partner. Concepts and tools such as these can be used to understand roles in an information society and others with whom we live and coexist, to understand the social structures—descendants of the primitive clans and tribes—that organize their lives, and, with an eye to the future, to design new organizations that are better equipped to cope with problems of the emerging age.

Beyond specific needs, there are many new challenges facing decision makers. Society will depend on the conceptual for the new visions and the flow of innovations required to cope with the pace and quantity of change. The leaders of the information age must reach out further into the universe and deeper into themselves to find creative solutions to modern-day problems. The directive will be saddled with the responsibility for making decisions that deal with the concrete practicality of everyday life in a confusing world of diversity and complexity. We must rely on the modern-day "Hunter" to guide and focus us as we embark on this new journey. We must also look to the analytical for the reasoning and analysis to formulate problems from the chaos we face and dispassionately sift through alternatives until an appropriate solution can be reached. For this, the "Headman" of the information age will have a large body of scientific knowledge and a vast array of computer and communications technology to draw upon. And herein lies the danger. For, in striving to more effectively cope with technology amidst complexity, it will be easy to ignore the human element. We may lose the essence of societal values and what it means to be human. The responsibility for avoiding this rests with the behavioral, who in this new world will become the keeper of society's heart and the forger of emotional bonds. The task of the "Clown" and the "Comforter" in the information society is to see that the heart remains strong and that humanity remains intact as we undergo all of these changes.

Analytical, conceptual, directive, and behavioral: all will assume important roles in the emerging environment of the information age as our jobs, personal needs, and social settings undergo change. There will be a richer array of styles and capacities available to deal with the changes in the four forces, but the job of matching them will become ever more difficult. The language of style can serve as a guide to help us uncover our hidden potential for success and to find alignment in this challenging era.

Style and the Future of Management

Why is concern so often expressed about the future of American management? In part, this concern reflects the impressive advances that have been made by Japan and other advanced countries. The wave of literature on what constitutes "excellent" management illustrates a number of interesting trends. It clearly points up the relevance of decision styles in dealing with managerial and organizational requirements to meet the coming onslaught of new environmental demands.

The cause of organizational malaise was studied by Peters and Waterman (1982) in their study of excellence in management. They focused on identifying the "innovative" companies and found that those companies had a sharp sense of the changes taking place in the environment and were especially good at responding to those changes. Using the eight measures of excellence that they developed, we will examine how they compare with corresponding decision styles.

1. A bias for action. This style avoids the classic "paralysis by analysis" syndrome. It corresponds to the directive and behavioral styles.
2. Staying close to the customers by understanding their needs for quality, service, and reliability and by listening to their new product ideas. This is characteristic of the directive.
3. Maintaining autonomy and leadership—encouraging creative individuals by not holding them back and allowing them the opportunity to try and fail. This corresponds to the conceptual.
4. Facilitating "productivity through people." Respect for the individual is what encourages excellent ideas and commitment. This reflects the perspective of the conceptual and the behavioral styles.
5. Being "hands-on value driven." Maintaining close contact with what is important in operations is a classic picture of the directive.
6. Knowing your business. Sticking to your knitting leads to excellent performance resulting from intimate knowledge of the business. This is most like the analytical.
7. Commitment from assuming responsibility. When the staff is kept simple and lean, the individual performs more effectively. Whereas the analytical favors elaborate reports, large staffs, and complex procedures, the directive prefers simple, direct, "bottom-line" results.
8. Having "simultaneous loose-tight properties." There is a need for both freedom of operation to achieve innovative operations and recognition that complete freedom can also mean chaos. This balanced perspective is typical of the conceptual.

Our study of the successful executive in a wide range of industries and types of business showed that those with the "conceptual/directive" style are indeed the most likely to be excellent executives. From our perspective, success is not measured solely by financial indicators but rather includes factors such as growth, competitiveness, ability to attract and retain excellent individuals, innovation, quality, responsiveness, adaptability, and social responsibility. Thus, the "bottom line," while important, does not by itself ensure "excellence in management." Rather, it is the combination of "vision and doing" that leads to effective organizational performance.

John Naisbitt (1982) identified ten major changes that would influence future business, such as an emphasis on information, high technology, a world economy, and a greater use of participation. We are clearly entering an era of increased ambiguity, complexity, and turbulence. The new society will require its best brains to compete effectively in a world market. The style that fits this requirement best is a combination of the analytical and the conceptual. The analytical is good at understanding extremely complex phenomena and translating these into meaningful data or information. The conceptual is also able to handle ambiguity easily and is able to see the implications of future possibilities. Dealing with future complexity will require leadership that focuses on freedom of expression and fosters achievement rather than repression. But how can a leader be at the same time both strong, and compassionate in regard to the needs and aspirations of others? Bennis and Nanus (1985), through the results of their interviews of ninety executives, have shown that the ability to create vision and the energy that initiates and sustains the actions make a vision become a reality through "transformative leadership." The leaders with a combination of the conceptual, directive, and behavioral styles are the leaders who can move organizations to new heights in dealing with potential opportunities while instilling within employees the commitment and energy needed to effectuate the possibilities. The conceptual has the vision, the directive has the energy and skill at exercising power, and the behavioral has the empathy and skill at making people feel involved.

In a study of vanguard management, O'Toole (1985) asked a subjective question during personal interviews with over 200 managers. The simple question was, "If you could choose to work in any large American corporation, which would it be?" Having identified eight such companies, O'Toole then went about determining what characteristics made them "vanguard companies." He found that they were people oriented, had visible leaders, planned for employee stability, had a consumer orientation, were future oriented, provided every worker a sense of ownership, and proved to be a link to small entrepreneurial businesses. Vanguard companies clearly employ a combination of the conceptual and directive styles.

Organizations that were not considered vanguard also appeared to have much in common. They were insensitive to the external environment, lost sight of the basics, and were both complacent and overly action oriented, while ignoring the need for change. They pursued short-term goals with single-minded leadership, especially where they were run by "left brained engineers." The limitations of a purely directive executive who is "too focused" on the situation at hand and end results become painfully clear. Insufficient attention is paid to the broad issues confronting the firm, and even less interest is displayed regarding needs of the workers.

O'Toole studied vanguard companies for three years and found that they all displayed concern about stakeholders, a dedication to high purpose, a willingness to adapt to new conditions, and a commitment to be the best in what they do. These four characteristics reflect a combination of the analytical and conceptual styles. This was the second most frequent style that we found in our interviews with executives. Among the eight companies originally identified as vanguard, several have since had difficulties. Perhaps vanguard companies also need a directive component to assure that their lofty ideals can indeed be successfully carried out.

Another perspective on the issue of what makes an excellent corporate manager is described in the book *Decision Making at the Top* (Donaldson and Lorsch, 1983). An in-depth interview with twelve chief executive officers gave Donaldson and Lorsch the material needed to find what executives consider as major factors in their decision making. As top management, they felt that they should be paid well, and they felt a commitment to doing well for the shareholders in the company. None of the executives was concerned about the current market value of the company's stock. What was important to most of them was the "drive to excel," to do better than others. As one executive put it, "My personal goals are to do a good job, to be profitable, to have high calibre people around me, and to be concerned about how I am viewed by customers, stockholders and the community. My objective is to be number one, to do as well or better than anyone else" (p. 22). This quotation would appear to come from a leader in a vanguard company. The underlying theme revealed was that executives are concerned with pride, competition, and excellence in performance. Because the executives interviewed were at the top of their respective companies, their competitiveness seemed to focus on how well they were doing as compared with other companies rather than as compared with peers inside the company. Having reached the pinnacle of their careers, they now had to reconcile their earlier dreams with the reality of what they might still be able to accomplish. Corporate survival was the dominant motivator of the CEO. People, ideas, and products were all part of the single most important objective: perpetuating the firm. The analytical/conceptual style appears to dominate, with a backup directive style expressed as a focus on achieving a single objective.

We can compare decision making at the top level with that at the lower levels by recognizing that aspiring managers struggle to reach higher positions in the firm. This was observed in our survey of eighty executives. Those at the vice-president and director levels were more analytical/conceptual than those at either the president or CEO/chair levels. These latter two levels were both predominantly entrepreneurial; that is, conceptual/directive. The Donaldson and Lorsch study would seem to confirm these findings in that the objectives identified by the presidents included the desire for both good financial performance and personal achievement. Their concerns for a balance among stakeholders agrees with O'Toole's findings. The survival objective and desire to remain independent by avoiding unfriendly takeovers is indicative of the conceptual style. Again we find a merging of research, all of which points to a style of management that is required to achieve excellence in the future environment that will confront management.

Undoubtedly, Japanese companies have demonstrated what many consider as excellence in management. But what accounts for the success of well-run Japanese firms? What we see is the great natural talent of the founder or chief executive who has an intuitive grasp of the basic elements of strategy, a way of looking at the company, customers, and competition that allows all of these to be merged into a comprehensive set of plans and objectives. The process is both creative and intuitive and often is disruptive of the status quo. It is the drive, the will, and the mind of the chief executive that gives these strategies the extraordinary competitive impact that we have observed. Here is a clear example of the conceptual style at work.

Ohmae (1982) identified four basic strategies that are used by Japanese management. They dissect the market, build on relative superiority, exploit strategic degrees of freedom, and apply strategic vision. The way in which Japanese executives make decisions discloses a very effective style. The mind of the Japanese strategist is creative, intuitive, and committed, with the drive and the energy to carry out difficult decisions. It is almost a picture-perfect copy of the entrepreneur. It is little wonder, then, that in the United States we have begun to recognize the need for more innovative companies, for vanguard companies, and for greater support for the intrapreneur and the entrepreneur.

What can we say about the executive of the future, given our current research base and future requirements regarding the new role of the entrepreneurial executive? To address this question, we will have to once again resort to using the four force model, for all executive decisions are made in an organizational context. Zaleznick (1977), for example, contends that few managers make rational decisions but rather that personalities and politics play the overriding role in determining the final outcome of decisions. Rituals of participation or sharing of power are considered unrealistic. What really determines the basis for decisions in an organization is consolidation of power around the executive, who becomes a central figure to whom members of the organization can form emotional attachments. Unless we are dealing with a tyrant, most decisions involve persuasion, negotiation, and concessions as means of obtaining support, and there are few cases of executives making decisions through a so-called formal mechanism. Who, then, is the persuader? Typically, the style that is most effective at persuasion is the conceptual/behavioral. In a large aerospace company, a division director with this style was able to retain the loyalty of his staff despite successive cuts in the organization that required transfers to other divisions. In a Ciba-Giegy subsidiary that had been for sale for over a year, the conceptual/behavioral manager was able to hold the key executives together because of his understanding of their needs and his ability to express confidence in the outcome of the sale. In another example, a department chair at a large metropolitan university was able to change the structure and the responsibilities of the faculty so that what had been considered an onerous task became a desired and sought-after responsibility. What emerges from these examples is that the highly directive style that has dominated American industry is not by itself sufficient to meet the new challenges confronting management.

Tandem Computers is an example of a highly successful company with very informal management. The philosophy is to treat people as the most important ingredient and then give them the support and the incentives to achieve outstanding performance. Control is self-control, where individual workers do not require constant monitoring. At Tandem, individual style "matches" the organizational requirement. The job gets done while the needs of the individuals in the organization are met.

To answer the question of who will manage the managers, we have to look at the shareholders and boards of directors in an organization. If the organization of today is truly a dinosaur, T. Boone Pickens may be right when he says that current managers are more interested in administrative procedures, perks, and tremendous salaries than in looking after stockholders' interests. What he is suggesting is that we need more entrepreneurial spirit to overcome mediocre management and to take advantage of opportunities. Rosabeth Moss Kanter (1982) claims that a new breed of American manager is starting to replace those who stubbornly cling to formulas, products, and marketing strategies that have long lost their appeal. This new breed is being called the innovators. They combine innovative management with discipline to focus initiative on the common goals and are rewarded for being collaborative. This message is similar to the argument that what will make the organization of the future different is the intrapreneur—the innovator and risk taker inside the organization, the maverick who does not seem to fit company rules yet is able to exploit opportunities and bring about major changes in how organizations are managed.

The spirit of individual enterprise can motivate the latent talents of many of today's managers. The military also are recognizing the potential of harnessing these latent talents. Admiral Crowe, recently appointed to chair the Joint Chiefs of Staff, is described by his friends as looking like an unmade bed. He makes jokes about how unmilitary he looks, but he is able to build rapport and shows an ability to exercise finesse in difficult situations. His congenial outlook along with his ability as a "strategic thinker" give him a head start on one of the toughest jobs in the military.

What does all this add up to? In the past, dogmatic, directive management was considered the style most effective in dealing with recalcitrant workers. Today, with a better educated work force, greater mobility, and greater achievement motives, management can no longer rely on what worked in the past. Politics, power, and dogmatic approaches will not disappear overnight. They will simply be overtaken by the entrepreneurial spirit, energy, and vision that have allowed companies such as Honda to challenge and overtake prestigious auto makers.

Style must be recognized as playing an important role in determining the likelihood of success for organizations yet to emerge. The innovative organization, the vanguard organization, and the entrepreneurial organization all require the same style of management—the dominant conceptual/directive, with either an analytical or a behavioral backup style, depending on the organizational requirements. We believe that this style of manager is the one most likely to lead organizations to a new level of competitive effectiveness and to be the excellent executive of the future.

Appendix A

●‖●

Validation of the Decision
Style Inventory

The usefulness of a decision style test instrument is directly related to how well it measures style and whether that measurement can be used to predict, with an acceptable level of accuracy, the expected behaviors related to a given style. To validate the Decision Style Inventory, extensive testing has been done over a number of years with different groups. The results of this testing confirm that the Decision Style Inventory can be used with a high level of confidence to determine an individual's decision style as well as the patterns that determine brain dominance and the behavior that can be expected for each pattern.

A number of statistical tests were used to determine the validity and reliability of the Decision Style Inventory:

1. Split-half reliability testing using nine groups from different organizations.
2. Test/retest reliability using different groups.
3. Item analysis of the instrument.
4. Correlation with other test instruments, notably the Myers-Briggs Type Indicator.
5. Face validity based on (a) personal interviews and (b) observations in longitudinal studies in organizations.
6. Comparisons of performance in various occupations with style pattern.

The results have proved highly significant. For example, there is a strong positive correlation with the Myers-Briggs, as well as other test instruments, such as the Wilkens Imbedded Figures Test, the Kolb Learning Style Inventory, and the Hermann Brain Dominance Instrument.

Face validity comparing an individual's self-perception with the results of the DSI is in the 90 percent range, as demonstrated in interviews with well over 1,000 individuals. Some of the individuals were in occupations that did not correspond with those predicted by their DSI scores. In almost every such instance, this discrepancy could be explained by other factors. For example, a professor with an extremely low behavioral score who claimed that he ''hated students'' said that he did not teach but was engaged in research and thus did not interact with students. An engineering professor who had a very low analytical score but a high conceptual style had previously studied to be a priest, and engineering was a second choice for him. Numerous examples such as these confirm that the DSI evokes an appropriate psychological response and provides people with a keen insight into their real preferences. In our longitudinal studies, we found that people whose styles did not fit their positions eventually either resigned or were transferred to new positions.

Analysis of the Department of Defense Study

In order to evaluate the potential of the DSI for government application, studies were undertaken with individual agencies or branches of the government as well as commercial organizations. In addition to these studies, other independent evaluations have been done; for example, the Army Research Institute has tested the DSI with brigadier generals. A number of other studies have been undertaken at various hospitals around the country. The results reported below are based on the study done by Hane, Rowe, and Boulgarides (1984) using a sample of 428 individuals from nine organizations: the Defense Systems Management College ($N = 33$); the Navy Personnel Group ($N = 42$); the Office of Naval Research ($N = 98$); Army Information Research ($N = 14$); the Navy Training Group ($N = 34$); an aerospace company ($N = 30$); the Southern California Association of Governments ($N = 29$); a Los Angeles managerial group ($N = 22$); and middle managers in the California State University ($N = 126$). The statistical analyses performed included (1) determination of the statistical relationships among the four basic styles of the inventory, (2) examination of the relationships between a given style and each of the twenty questions (item analysis), (3) examination of the intercorrelations between two split halves for each style, and (4) determination of normality of the distribution of the data for each style. The mean scores and the standard deviations were calculated for the four styles for the total sample of 428, as shown in Table 14.

Table 14. Mean Values for the Composite Sample of 428 Individuals.

	Mean Values	Standard Deviation
Directive	78.0	15.3
Analytical	90.5	16.5
Conceptual	74.8	15.2
Behavioral	56.6	15.5

Scores were also calculated for subgroups based on sex and age (62 percent of the sample were men and 38 percent women; 61 percent of the subjects were under age forty). Comparisons were made between mean scores of men and women and between mean scores of the younger and older individuals. The mean scores for the different groups were very similar, and tests of statistical significance revealed that none of the means differed at the 5 percent significance level. This supports our findings regarding female managers described in Chapter Seven. The means and standard deviations are shown in Table 15.

Alternate scoring approaches were reported by Mann (1982). These ranged from simple ranking using values of 1, 2, 3, and 4 to a complex, open-ended weighting scheme that allowed the use of any single-digit number. The results showed that the style categories were not significantly affected by open scoring and that the geometric scoring of the DSI has the advantage of indicating style profiles on the basis of norms for a large number of individuals who have been tested. The forced

Table 15. Means and Standard Deviations
for Total Sample and Subgroups.

	Total (N = 428)	Men (N = 141)	Women (N = 86)	Under Age 40 (N = 139)	Age 40 and Over (N = 86)
Directive					
Mean	78.0	79.2	79.9	78.9	80.5
Standard deviation	15.3	13.7	17.0	15.3	14.5
Analytical					
Mean	90.5	87.4	88.3	87.2	88.8
Standard deviation	16.5	14.1	15.7	14.0	15.8
Conceptual					
Mean	74.8	75.0	71.9	74.2	72.7
Standard deviation	15.2	14.4	16.0	14.9	15.0
Behavioral					
Mean	56.6	58.3	59.9	59.7	57.9
Standard deviation	15.5	16.1	15.3	15.3	16.6

Note: Not all individuals who took the DSI indicated their sex or age.

ranking appears to evoke a response that more correctly measures a person's decision style. Rowe and Boulgarides (1983) reported that the Decision Style Inventory has a face validity of well over 90 percent and reliability of 70 percent. These statistical measures would indicate that the DSI is a valid test instrument.

Relationships Among Scales

Correlation coefficients among the four styles revealed a strong pattern of relationship, consistent throughout the samples. The correlations of one style with the other styles are almost entirely negative, with only a very few small positive correlations. This pattern of relationship demonstrates one of the important characteristics of the Decision Style Inventory. Each of the four styles is independent of the others. On the basis of this finding, one can state with a high level of confidence that a person's decision style will not depend on which one of the styles is dominant and which are backup.

Relationship Between Styles and Instrument Questions

The score for each style is the total of the responses to the twenty individual items in each column. To examine how individual items contributed to determination of the style, each of the items was correlated with the total style score. The correlation coefficients indicate the extent to which a particular item contributed to the total score. The scores for 95 percent of the items on each scale were statistically significant and had reasonably high correlation coefficients with the corresponding total style score. Only five out of the eighty items on the instrument had correlations of less than .15 (6 percent), and only two of the items (2.5 percent) had correlations of less than .10. The results show that the questions and the responses appropriately measure each individual style.

Intercorrelations Between Split Halves of Each Style

For this analysis, the items were split into two halves of ten items each, the odd-numbered items in one half and the even-numbered items in the other half. Total scores were then calculated for each half of the style, one from each of the two sets of ten items. Each style was then correlated with the two scores. The correlations were corrected for test length, using the Spearman-Brown formula. This analysis provided an indication of the internal consistency of each of the styles. This is one of the methods used to estimate reliability. The correlation coefficients ranged from .5 to .7 for the split-half test.

These split-half correlation coefficients should be interpreted in terms of purpose, design, and use of the inventory. The instrument was not designed so that each item measured exactly the same property as every other item. Therefore, internal consistency (high correlations among the items of a style) would not necessarily be expected, although a coefficient of .7 is considered highly appropriate for this design. Another important consideration in using split-half analysis is that a twenty-item instrument yields two ten-item halves. This small number limits the construct validity of split-half results, especially considering that Ipsitive scoring creates interdependencies among the four styles. Thus, we examined the patterns of scores for all four styles, in addition to the split-half correlations for each separate style.

Another measure of reliability that was used was a test-retest procedure. This approach also showed a 0.7 correlation, examining the pattern among the four styles. That is, if all four styles were unchanged when the test was retaken, it was considered reliable. Fifteen percent of the individuals who retook the test showed a change in one style category, and another 15 percent showed a change in two or more categories.

Reliability and Validity of the Myers-Briggs Type Indicator

McCaulley (1981) summarized the extensive literature on internal consistency and test-retest reliability of the separate scales and type classifications for the Myers-Briggs Type Inventory (MBTI). She noted that reliability data are available in the MBTI manual (Myers, 1976, p. 20) and that review articles show that coefficients are highly acceptable. McCaulley also noted that when changes of type occur on retest, most changes affect just one preference, usually the one with the lowest original score. Test stability was confirmed in test-retest studies by a number of individuals and has been summarized by McCaulley (1981).

McCaulley offered extensive current information on studies of construct validity, and she categorized the findings in the areas of predictions about specific types, type differences in career choices, and creativity. Validity was based on correlations of continuous scores with other measures. In studies of the MBTI's utility as a predictor of college students' choices of major and college success, the MBTI has a moderate predictive validity.

In reviewing Myers-Briggs normative information, Dickel (1983) noted that preference scores are not centered around a mean of zero and that the thinking/feeling (*TF*) dimension seems biased toward thinking. He reported a "relatively high" standard deviation when compared with the means, indicating a fairly wide dispersion of scores. In considering sex differences in score distribution, Dickel reported higher scores for males on the thinking dimension, and he related this to a similar significant difference in the behavioral style on the Decision Style Inventory, stating that "females also tend to be more extroverted, sensing and judging than males" (p. 125). Dickel also described a distribution of the four Jungian types by sex. He noted that 76.5 percent of his sample falls into either *ST* or *NT* categories. Only about a third of subjects were feeling types, and proportionately more of these were females. He concludes that the differences between males and females is particularly notable in the *ST-NT* distinction. Using a procedure similar to discriminant analysis, Dickel concluded that the Myers-Briggs Type Indicator "works well in discriminating between types" (p. 129); in applying a similar procedure to the Decision Style Inventory, he concluded that the DSI results in "very robust measurements."

Coan's (1978) review of the MBTI noted that it consists of 166 well-designed items with apparent construct validity, and the overall score patterns correlate with esthetic and vocational preferences, aptitudes, needs, creativity, academic achievement, and work habits. Liabilities include Stricker and Ross's (1964) finding that the scales are not truly bipolar, orthogonal, or independent. As was noted, the judging/perceiving (*JP*) dimension departs from Jung's (1923) original construct and has "dubious validity."

Cross Validation of the Myers-Briggs Type Indicator and the Decision Style Inventory

In Dickel's (1983) cross validation of the Myers-Briggs Type Indicator with the Decision Style Inventory, he concluded that a test of independence shows a highly significant relationship between the two tests. In an analysis of variance of the Decision Style Inventory scores with the Myers-Briggs Type Inventory scores, Dickel concluded that the two instruments are conceptually consistent. The directive type most resembles the *ST* type and is least like the *NT* type. He used these data to support his hypothesis that *ST* types have short-range orientation for a single goal, are fairly autocratic in decision making, and favor centralized, well-defined tasks and organizational structures. He related the analytical type to both the *NT* and *ST* types, finding them least similar to the *SF* types. The analyticals display little emotion in decision making and prefer elaborate planning models prepared by experts, detailed calculations, and contingency plans. The conceptual type is most similar to the *NF* and *NT* and least like the *SF*. He stated that this finding supports his hypothesis that these individuals are speculative and intuitive, have a long-range focus, and favor decentralized decision making. The behavioral style most resembles the *SF* type and is least similar to the *NT* type. People of this type prefer participative decision making aided by experts' planning, and their decision validation is based on acceptance by others rather than on performance. Dickel's findings are summarized in Table 16.

Table 16. Comparison of Average DSI Scores with MBTI Types.

	Directive	*Analytical*	*Conceptual*	*Behavioral*
SF type	75.81[a]	73.94	73.69	76.56[a]
ST type	76.17[a]	90.08[a]	74.52	59.07
NF type	68.67	77.26	90.93[a]	63.13[a]
NT type	68.48	92.81[a]	84.27[a]	54.43
Total	72.78	87.64	79.42	60.08
Analysis of variance (ANOVA), *P* value (between groups)	.0343	.0006	.0003	.0000

[a]Positive correlation.

Source: Dickel, 1983, p. 132.

Dickel investigated other relations between the two instruments when he categorized the decision style types on the introversion-extroversion dimension and concluded that "lower-half types" in the Decision Style Inventory tend to be more extroverted than the upper-half types. He also noted that the conceptual style favors perceiving, whereas the analytical and behavioral styles favor judging.

Mann's (1982) research also compared the MBTI with the Decision Style Inventory. He noted that there are nonlinear biases affecting the strength of the judging/perceiving *(JP)* and introvert/extrovert *(IE)* dimensions. He asserted that a strong judging and/or introvert bias will tend to orient the MBTI so that the sensing/thinking *(ST)* process would match the directive *(D)* in the DSI. The intuitive/thinking *(NT)* process will then match the analytical *(A)* of the DSI. For example, a style designation of *ENTP* for the MBTI will be very close in quality to that of a dominant conceptual *(C)* for the DSI. Mann also hypothesized the likely relation between the two instruments for various personality characteristics, as shown in Table 17. Because the MBTI is a bipolar instrument, the corresponding two dimensions in the DSI can be readily related.

Table 17. Relation Between DSI and MBTI Types on Selected Personality Characteristics.

Personality	DSI	MBTI
Proactive	A, C	E, N
Adaptive	A, C	E, N
Change oriented	A, C	E, N
Evaluative	A, C	I, S
Reactive	D, B	I, S
Rules oriented	D, B	T, S
Maintenance	D, B	T, S
Verbal	D, B	N, E
Logical	D, A	T, S
Analytical	D, A	T, S
Speed oriented	D, B	F, N
Intuitive	C	F, N
People oriented	C, B	E, N, F
Task oriented	D, A	I

Note: A = analytical; *B* = behavioral; *C* = conceptual; *D* = directive; *E* = extrovert; *I* = introvert; *T* = thinking; *F* = feeling; *S* = sensing; *N* = intuiting.

Craft (1984, pp. 144–145) also examined the relationship between the MBTI and DSI categories. He noted that the *ST* individual relies mainly on facts and makes decisions using impersonal analysis of serial, logical reasoning. This corresponds to the directive style of the Decision Style Inventory. The *NF* person tends to rely on intuition for perceiving and prefers feeling as the basis of judging. This type is often warm and more interested in facts about people than about things, corresponding to the DSI's conceptual category. The *NT* individual uses intuition for perception but tends to focus on technical, impersonal analysis, as in the analytical style. Finally, the *SF* person prefers feelings, focuses on people, and finds communication and interaction easy. This last category is comparable to the behavioral in the DSI model. Craft's data showed that of twelve analyticals in his study, five were *NT* and 5 *ST*. Of the eleven directives, he found that six were *ST* and three *SF*.

Conclusions

A primary objective of the Department of Defense research was to determine the reliability and validity of the Decision Style Inventory. The populations measured were quite diverse, including industry managers, defense contractors, and civil service and military service personnel. In spite of this range of occupation, age, and sex, the distribution of mean scores remained fairly stable.

Additional analyses showed that there are no significant differences between the mean or median scores. Thus, using the mean and standard deviation, based on a normal distribution, is appropriate. There was no significant difference between male and female scores, which corroborates other data on sex differences. Finally, the instrument has a high level of correlation with tests such as the Myers-Briggs that have been used for many years and is a valid instrument.

Appendix B

●‖●

Results: A Study
of Senior Executives

The data shown in Tables 18 through 21 are representative of individuals in a wide range of industries and include male and female executives. These data were collected from the eighty executives described in Chapter Eight (Table 13). Each of the individual executives was interviewed and given the DSI test instrument. Because the instrument is self-scoring, the results were presented to each executive and explained briefly when they completed the inventory. Then the results were input on a personal computer using a computer program developed by Rowe and Cox (1986). The final evaluation was returned to the executives for their review and comment. While no formal validation was undertaken, the executives who responded to their final evaluation were in agreement with the results.

The results are included here for two principal reasons. First, it is rare that raw data are made available for use by others and, second, by including these data any individual can compare his or her score with those of the executives tested. The sample is sufficient to provide a useful base for analysis and to illustrate that there is a range of patterns of style, all of which fit the positions in Tables 18 through 21.

Table 18. Decision Styles of Corporate Chairpersons.

Executive	Position	Directive	Analytical	Conceptual	Behavioral
1	Chairperson	89	90	81	44
2	Chairperson	49	111	100	40

Table 18. Decision Styles of Corporate Chairpersons, Cont'd.

Executive	Position	Directive	Analytical	Conceptual	Behavioral
3	Chairperson	70	87	107	40
4	Chairperson	71	85	96	52
5	Chairperson	73	86	100	38
6	Chairperson	79	88	84	49
7	Chairperson	86	93	67	64
8	Chairperson and CEO	71	110	96	37
9	Board chairperson	50	60	97	89
10	Retired chairperson	79	82	90	49

Table 19. Decision Styles of Company Presidents.

Executive	Position	Directive	Analytical	Conceptual	Behavioral
1	President	82	87	96	35
2	President	69	80	88	63
3	President	90	85	82	43
4	President and CEO	60	112	79	60
5	President of two corporations	68	92	91	49
6	President	60	86	105	49
7	President	86	105	75	34
8	President	86	85	91	35
9	President and CEO	88	77	88	47
10	President	86	74	88	52
11	President	85	72	89	54
12	President	86	81	95	48
13	President	94	75	87	44
14	President	70	70	103	57
15	President	68	108	76	47
16	President	58	92	105	45
17	President	47	91	125	37
18	President	71	72	97	60
19	President and CEO	82	89	70	66
20	President	66	92	86	55
21	President	101	105	58	36
22	President	99	73	71	57
23	President and chairperson	91	101	69	39
24	Retired president and CEO	112	78	64	46
25	President and chairperson	82	74	97	40
26	President and chairperson	71	71	111	47
27	CEO	60	115	84	41
28	CEO	76	72	93	59
29	President	49	78	119	56
30	President	69	75	99	48
31	President and CEO	82	89	70	66
32	President	80	100	92	28

Table 20. Decision Styles of Company Vice-Presidents.

Executive	Position	Directive	Analytical	Conceptual	Behavioral
1	Vice-president for strategic planning	70	77	107	46
2	Executive vice-president	82	94	108	32
3	Vice-president of law firm	85	93	69	53
4	Vice-president	68	109	87	36
5	Vice-president of national division	70	96	84	50
6	Executive vice-president	71	90	105	34
7	Vice-president	64	97	87	60
8	Corporate controller	50	108	96	46
9	Staff vice-president	56	119	73	52
10	Senior vice-president	60	120	95	27
11	Vice-president	70	96	84	50
12	Vice-president	54	111	89	46
13	Vice-president	69	96	84	50
14	Vice-president	83	87	94	36
15	Vice-president	85	70	98	47
16	Senior vice-president	52	117	86	43
17	Vice-president	63	80	117	55
18	Vice-president	73	69	98	58
19	Vice-president	75	94	76	55
20	Vice-president	67	99	75	59
21	Vice-president	61	107	88	44
22	Vice-president	70	87	86	57

Table 21. Decision Styles of Company Directors and Managers.

Executive	Position	Directive	Analytical	Conceptual	Behavioral
1	Director, advance planning	95	98	76	21
2	Manager, advance planning	52	65	125	58
3	Manager, resource planning	80	93	80	47
4	Manager	69	75	99	48
5	Manager	35	108	112	47
6	Director	61	73	110	56
7	Director of corporate planning	48	84	102	68
8	Director	70	90	96	45
9	Director	79	83	104	26
10	Director	68	94	96	45
11	Director	72	70	97	61
12	Director	60	107	103	34
13	Director	83	100	85	32
14	Director	82	69	104	45
15	Director	63	83	91	63
16	Dean	69	68	108	46

Appendix C

●II●II●II●II●II●II●II●II●II●II●II●II●II●II●II●II●II●II●II●II●II●II●II●II●II●II●II●II●II●II●II●II●

Results: A Study
of Entrepreneurs

In 1984, Jeffrey A. Hansen (1985) undertook a study of the decision styles of chief executive officers at emerging companies. The purpose of the study was to show the relationship between the styles of successful executives and the stage of development of the company. Hansen found that when there was a mismatch between the company's stage of development and the style of the chief executive officer the firms failed to attract venture capital funding. He also found that firms funded by venture capitalists showed slow growth when the styles of their chief executives were significantly less analytical in the second stage of development. The results of Hansen's study are summarized in Tables 22, 23, and 24.

Table 22. Decision Styles of CEOs and Companies' Stage of Development.

Stage of Development	Number of Employees	Most Effective Decision Style
1. Concept development	1–9	High conceptual Low analytical
2. Company development	10–25	High analytical High behavioral Low conceptual Low directive
3. Company positioning	26–75	High conceptual Low behavioral
4. Process operation	75 or more	High directive

Source: Hansen, 1985. Reprinted by permission.

202

The DSI scores of successful entrepreneurs are shown in Table 23. These executives had styles that matched the development stage of their company. Table 24 includes the DSI scores of entrepreneurs whose styles did not match the development stage of their company and who had less success in achieving growth or attracting venture capital. These results were reported in *Working Woman* ("How to Manage a Growing Company," 1987).

Of the fifty-nine chief executive officers tested, the twenty-four whose scores are shown in Table 23 had the successful entrepreneurial style, a combination of conceptual and directive. Of the thirty-five executives whose scores are shown in Table 24, only 34 percent had the successful entrepreneurial style. An article in *Business Week* echoes these ideas; it states that the entrepreneur who brings new products to market is the wrong person to manage a mature product ("Matching Managers to a Company's Life Cycle," 1981).

The important lesson from this study is aptly summarized by Drucker (1984, p. 68) who claims, "The most important economic event of the last few years is the rousing success of young companies founded on basic management practices." He indicates that of the 20 million new jobs created in the past decade, most are in small, new enterprises.

Table 23. Decision Styles of Successful Entrepreneurs.

Entrepreneur	Directive	Analytical	Conceptual	Behavioral
1	78	86	94	42
2	87	85	79	49
3	82	62	120	36
4	92	67	87	54
5	74	79	107	40
6	80	73	99	48
7	81	47	117	55
8	70	75	119	36
9	95	81	75	119
10	89	50	114	47
11	92	79	84	45
12	76	92	81	51
13	85	89	87	36
14	80	69	115	36
15	79	80	93	43

Table 23. Decision Styles of Successful Entrepreneurs, Cont'd.

Entrepreneur	Directive	Analytical	Conceptual	Behavioral
16	70	80	113	37
17	79	79	110	32
18	80	68	93	59
19	77	91	86	46
20	91	74	97	38
21	86	94	82	38
22	95	57	89	59
23	80	88	90	42
24	88	85	93	34
Average	83	76	97	44

Source: Hansen, 1985. Reprinted by permission.

Table 24. Decision Styles of Less Successful Entrepreneurs.

Entrepreneur	Directive	Analytical	Conceptual	Behavioral
1	68	69	91	72
2	67	82	85	66
3	59	104	89	48
4	85	85	66	64
5	65	65	91	79
6	59	105	95	41
7	65	79	99	57
8	76	95	98	31
9	81	94	69	56
10	84	104	77	35
11	60	74	101	65
12	69	88	89	54
13	86	92	75	47
14	69	79	72	80
15	66	97	70	67
16	55	72	111	62
17	77	50	101	72
18	82	110	60	48
19	76	72	65	87
20	76	105	86	33
21	66	63	94	77
22	57	106	94	43
23	82	95	71	52
24	73	72	84	71
25	76	89	98	37
26	66	73	104	57
27	46	95	81	78
28	67	119	69	45
29	73	97	84	46
30	42	68	106	84
31	89	97	74	40

Table 24. Decision Styles of Less Successful Entrepreneurs, Cont'd.

Entrepreneur	Directive	Analytical	Conceptual	Behavioral
32	86	113	67	34
33	93	79	66	62
34	55	106	83	56
35	94	77	69	60
Average	71	88	84	57

Source: Hansen, 1985. Reprinted by permission.

References

Ackoff, R. L. *The Art of Problem Solving*. New York: Wiley, 1978.

Ackoff, R. L., and Emery, F. E. *On Purposeful Systems*. Chicago: Aldine Atherton, 1972.

Adorno, T. W., Frankel-Brunswik, E., Levinson, D. J., and Sanford, R. N. *The Authoritarian Personality*. New York: Free Press, 1950.

Allport, G. W. *Personality: A Psychological Interpretation*. New York: Holt, Rinehart & Winston, 1937.

Andersen, K. "A Spunky Tycoon Turned Superstar." *Time*, Apr. 1, 1985, pp. 30–39.

Argyris, C. "The CEO's Behavior: Key to Organizational Development." *Harvard Business Review*, 1973, *51* (2), 53–64.

Baig, E. C. "America's Most Admired Corporations." *Fortune*, Jan. 19, 1987, pp. 18–31.

Bakan, P. "The Eyes Have It." *Psychology Today*, 1971, *4*, 64–69.

Barnard, C. I. *The Functions of the Executive*. Cambridge, Mass.: Harvard University Press, 1938.

Bello, F. "The Magic That Made Polaroid." *Fortune*, Apr. 1959, pp. 158.

Bennis, W. G. "Leadership: A Beleaguered Species?" *Organizational Dynamics*, 1976, *5* (1), 3–16.

Bennis, W. G. "Book Review of *Geneen* by Robert J. Schoenberg." *Los Angeles Times, Book Review*, May 5, 1985, p. 9.

Bennis, W. G., and Nanus, B. *Leaders: The Strategies for Taking Charge*. New York: Harper & Row, 1985.

"Big Boss of the Thunder Herd." *Life,* May 1967, p. 47.

"Big Shoes for the U.S. to Fill." *Life,* 1967, *63* (23), 35.

Binet, A. *Modern Ideas about Children.* Translated by Suzanne Heisler. Menlo Park, Calif.: Suzanne Heisler, 1984.

Blake, R., and Mouton, J. *Managerial Grid.* Houston: Gulf Publishing, 1965.

Boulgarides, J. D., and Rowe, A. J. "The Police Chief as a Decision Maker." *Journal of California Law Enforcement,* Winter 1983, pp. 1–5.

Briggs, K. C., and Myers, I. B. *Myers-Briggs Type Indicator (F).* Princeton, N.J.: Educational Testing Service, 1957.

Brousseau, K. R. "Toward a Dynamic Model of Job-Person Relationships: Findings, Research Questions, and Implications for Work System Design." *Academy of Management Review,* 1983, *8* (1), 33–45.

Bruner, J. S., Goodnow, J. J., and Austin, G. A. *A Study of Thinking.* New York: Wiley, 1956.

Burck, C. G. "A Group Profile of the Fortune 500 Chief Executive." *Fortune,* 1976, *93* (5), 173–177, 308–312.

Bylinsky, G. "America's Best-Managed Factories." *Fortune,* 1984, *109* (11), 16–24.

Carlsson, B., Keane, P., and Martin, B. J. "R&D Organizations as Learning Systems." *Sloan Management Review,* 1976, *17* (3), 1–15.

Carlyn, M. "An Assessment of the Myers-Briggs Type Indicator." *Journal of Personality Assessment,* 1977, *21,* 461–473.

Caro, R. A. *The Power Broker,* New York: Vintage, 1975.

Carskadon, T. G. "Test-Retest Reliabilities of Continuous Scores on the Myers-Briggs Type Indicator." *Psychological Reports,* 1977, *41,* 1011–1012.

Carskadon, T. G. "Clinical and Counseling Aspects of the Myers-Briggs Type Indicator." *Bulletin of Research in Psychological Type,* 1979, *2,* 2–31.

Cawly, R. H. "A Company Guide to Compensating Top Executives." Internal publication. *Price Waterhouse—Capsule Cases.* Spring/Summer 1985, p. 9.

Chakravarty, S. N. "What It Takes to Be an Entrepreneur." *Forbes,* Mar. 2, 1981, pp. 100–101.

Chang, Y. N. "Corporate Strategy." *The Executive,* Jul. 1981, pp. 11–12.

Coan, R. W. "Review of the Myers-Briggs Type Indicator." In D. K. Buros (ed.), *The Eighth Mental Measurements Yearbook.* Highland Park, N.J.: Gryphon, 1978.

Copeman, G. H. *The Chief Executive and Business Growth.* New York: Leviathan House, 1974.

Craft, C. J. "An Examination of the Decision Style in Tasks Using Accountant Information." Unpublished dissertation, University of Southern California, Nov. 1984.

Culbert, S. A., and McDonough, J. J. *The Invisible War: Pursuing Self-Interests at Work.* New York: Wiley, 1980.

Cyert, R. M., and March, J. G. *A Behavioral Theory of the Firm.* Englewood Cliffs, N.J.: Prentice-Hall, 1963.

Deal, T., and Kennedy, A. *Corporate Cultures.* Reading, Mass.: Addison-Wesley, 1984.

Dickel, K. E. *The Effect of Inquiry Mode and Decision Style on Strategic Decision-Making Behavior.* Los Angeles: University of Southern California, 1983.

Donaldson, G., and Lorsch, J. W. *Decision Making at the Top: The Shaping of Strategic Direction.* New York: Basic Books, 1983.

Driver, M. J., and Streufert, S. "Integrative Complexity." *Administrative Science Quarterly,* 1969, *14,* 272–285.

Drucker, P., "How New Entrepreneurs Are Challenging U.S. Business," *U.S. News and World Report,* Mar. 26, 1984, p. 68.

Drucker, P. "The Worst Thing Is to Modernize." *U.S. News & World Report,* Feb. 2, 1987, p. 23.

Elbing, A. *Behavioral Decisions in Organizations.* Glenview, Ill.: Scott, Foresman, 1970.

Emery, F. E., and Trist, E. L. "The Causal Texture of Organizational Environments." *Human Relations,* 1965, *18,* 21–32.

Fiedler, F. E. "Engineer the Job to Fit the Manager." *Harvard Business Review,* 1965, *43* (5), 115–122.

Franklin, B. *Poor Richard's Almanac.* New York: H. M. Caldwell, 1900. (Originally published 1758.)

Freud, S. *New Introductory Lectures on Psychoanalysis.* New York: Norton, 1933.

Freud, S. *The Ego and the Id.* London: Hogarth Press, 1947.

Freud, S. *The Interpretation of Dreams.* London: Hogarth Press, 1953.

Freud, S. *Group Psychology and the Analysis of the Ego.* New York: Liverright, 1967. (Originally published in German in 1921.)

Geneen, H. S. "The Case for Managing by the Numbers." *Fortune,* 1984, *110* (7), 78-81.

Goldstein, K. M., and Blackman, S. *Cognitive Style.* New York: Wiley, 1978.

Gordon, R. A., and Howell, J. E. *Higher Education for Business.* New York: Columbia University Press, 1959.

Grayson, C. J. "Management Science and Business Practice." *Harvard Business Review,* 1973, *51* (4), 41-50.

Greiner, L. E. "What Managers Think of Participative Management." *Harvard Business Review,* 1973, *51* (2), 111-117.

Grimsley, G., and Jarrett, H. F. "The Relation of Past Managerial Achievement to Test Measures Obtained in the Employment Situation." *Personnel Psychology,* 1973, *26,* 31-48.

Hall, T. "Executive Style." *Wall Street Journal,* Oct. 1, 1984, p. 1, 20.

Hane, E. Z., Rowe, A. J., and Boulgarides, J. D. "Statistical Analysis of the Decision Style Inventory, the Values Inventory and the Organization Culture Instruments." Unpublished report, U.S. Department of Defense, 1984. (MDA 903-84-M-8396)

Hansen, J. A., "CEO Management Style and the Stages of Development in New Ventures." Unpublished report, Atkinson Graduate School of Management, Williamette University, 1985.

"Harold Geneen's Tribulations." *Business Week,* Aug. 11, 1973, pp. 102-110.

Hayes, L. S. "What's Kodak Developing Now?" *Fortune,* 1981, *103* (6), 78-91.

Heidrick and Struggles, Inc. *The Profile of a President: Survey of*

Presidents of 471 of America's Largest Companies. Chicago: Heidrick and Struggles, Inc., 1967.

Hellriegel, D., and Slocum, J. W., Jr. "Managerial Problem-Solving Styles." *Business Horizons,* Dec. 1975, pp. 29–37.

"Here Comes the 'Intrapreneur.'" *Business Week,* Jul. 18, 1983, pp. 188–190.

Hersey, P., and Blanchard, K. *Management of Organizational Behavior.* Englewood Cliffs, N.J.: Prentice-Hall, 1972.

Hillman, J. *Revisioning Psychology.* New York: Harper & Row, 1975.

Homer, *The Illiad of Homer.* Edited by M. Mack. Translated by A. Pope. New Haven, Conn.: Yale University Press, 1967.

"How Executives Spend Their Time." *Creative Management Newsletter,* 1982, p. 2.

"How New Entrepreneurs Are Changing U.S. Business." *U.S. News & World Report,* Mar. 26, 1984, pp. 68–69.

"How to Manage a Growing Company." *Working Woman,* Apr. 1987, pp. 39–42.

Hudson, L. *Contrary Imaginations.* New York: Schocken Books, 1966.

Huysmans, J.H. *The Implementation of Operations to Research.* Operations Research Society of America Series no. 19. New York: Wiley, 1970.

Hymowitz, C. "Small Business Owners Discover Giving Up Authority Isn't Easy." *Wall Street Journal,* May 23, 1985, p. 23.

"Implementation of a Cognitive Skills Training Program in R.O.T.C.: The Leadership Enrichment Program." Unpublished report, Army Research Institute, 1987.

Isenberg, D. J. "How Senior Managers Think." *Harvard Business Review,* 1984, *62* (6), 81–90.

"ITT: The View from Inside." *Business Week,* November 3, 1973, pp. 43–48.

Jacobi, J. *The Psychology of C. G. Jung.* New Haven, Conn.: Yale University Press, 1973.

Janis, I., and Mann, L. *Decision-Making.* New York: Free Press, 1977.

Janis, I., and Wheeler, D. "Thinking Clearly about Career Choices." *Psychology Today,* May 1978, pp. 67–76, 121–122.

Jaques, E. *The Form of Time.* New York: Crane-Russak, 1982.

Johnson, C. R. "Of Group Decisions." *Dimensions/NBS,* May 1979, p. 3.

Jung, C. G. *Psychological Types.* New York: Pantheon Books, 1923.

Jung, C. G. *Psychological Types.* (Rev. ed.) New York: Pantheon Books, 1959.

Jung, C. G. *Analytical Psychology: Its Theory and Practice.* New York: Pantheon Books, 1968.

Jung, C. G. *Man and His Symbols.* New York: Doubleday, 1971.

Kanter, R. M. "The Middle Manager as Innovator," *Harvard Business Review,* 1982, *60* (4), 95–105.

Katz, R. L. "Skills of an Effective Administrator," *Harvard Business Review,* 1955, *33* (1), 33–42.

Keen, P.G.W. *The Implications of Cognitive Style for Individual Decision Making.* Cambridge, Mass.: Harvard Business School, 1973.

Kets de Vries, M.F.R., and Miller, D. *The Neurotic Organization: Diagnosing and Changing Counterproductive Styles of Management.* San Francisco: Jossey-Bass, 1984.

Kichen, S. "What It Takes to Stay on Top." *Forbes,* Nov. 5, 1984, pp. 128–129.

Kiechel, W., III. "Attack of the Obsessive Managers." *Fortune,* Feb. 16, 1987, pp. 127–128.

Kilman, R. H., and Mitroff, I. I. "Qualitative Versus Quantitative Analysis for Management Science." *Interfaces,* Feb. 1976, pp. 17–27.

Konner, M. "She & He." *Science,* Sept. 1982, pp. 54–61.

Kotter, J. P. *The General Manager.* New York: Free Press, 1982a.

Kotter, J. P. "What Effective General Managers Really Do." *Harvard Business Review,* 1982b, *60* (6), 156–167.

Lawler, E. *High Involvement Management.* San Francisco: Jossey-Bass, 1986.

Levinson, H. "Management by Whose Objectives." *Harvard Business Review,* 1970, *48* (4), 125–134.

Levinson, H. "The Abrasive Personality." *Harvard Business Review,* 1978, *56* (3), 86–94.

Levinson, H. *Executive.* Cambridge, Mass.: Harvard University Press, 1981.

Levinson, H. "A Second Career: The Possible Dream." *Harvard Business Review*, 1983, *61* (3), 122–129.

Lewin, K. *A Dynamic Theory of Personality*. New York: McGraw-Hill, 1935.

Lewin, K. *Principles of Topological Psychology*. New York: McGraw-Hill, 1936.

Lewin, K. *Topological Psychology*. New York: McGraw-Hill, 1938.

Lewin, K. *Field Theory and Social Science*. New York: Harper & Row, 1951.

Liebling, A. J. "Five-Star Schoolmaster." *New Yorker*, Mar. 10, 1951, p. 48.

Louis, A. M. "America's New Economy: How to Manage in It." *Fortune*, June 23, 1986, pp. 21–25.

Ludwig, S. "Management." *The Executive*, Feb. 1981, pp. 46–48.

McCaulley, M. H. "Jung's Theory of Psychological Types and the Myers-Briggs Type Indicator." *Advances in Psychological Assessment*, 1981, *5*, 194, 352.

McClelland, D. C. *The Achieving Society*. New York: Wiley, 1961.

McKenney, J. L., and Keen, P.G.W. "How Managers' Minds Work." *Harvard Business Review*, 1973, *51* (4), 79–90.

Maier, N.R.F. "Group Problem-Solving." *Psychological Review*, 1967, *74*, 239–249.

Mann, R. B. *Relationship Between Decision Styles of Corporate Planners and Other Planning Executives*. Los Angeles: University of Southern California, 1982.

Marrow, A. J. "Group Dynamics in Industry." Paper presented to the National Vocational Guidance Association Convention, Chicago, 1948.

Marrow, A. J. *Behind the Executive Mask*. New York: AMACOM, 1964.

Marrow, A. J. *The Practical Theorist*. New York: Basic Books, 1969.

Marrow, A. J. "Management by Participation." In E. L. Cass and F. G. Zimmer (eds), *Man and Work in Society*. New York: Van Nostrand Reinhold, 1975.

Maslow, A. *Motivation and Personality*. New York: Harper & Row, 1954.

Mason, R. O., and Mitroff, I. I. "A Program for Research on Management Information Systems." *Management Science,* 1973, *19* (5), 475–487.

Mason, R., Mitchell, R., Hamptom, W. J., and Frons, M. "Ross Perot's Crusade." *Business Week,* Oct. 6, 1986, pp. 60–65.

"Matching Managers to a Company's Life Cycle." *Business Week,* Feb. 23, 1981, pp. 62–74.

"Maybe I'm Worth $5 Million a Year." *Forbes,* May 15, 1971, pp. 186–190.

Mintzberg, H. *The Nature of Managerial Work.* New York: Harper & Row, 1973.

Mintzberg, H. "The Manager's Job: Folklore and Fact." *Harvard Business Review,* 1975, *53* (4), 49.

Mintzberg, H. "Planning on the Left Side and Managing on the Right." *Harvard Business Review,* 1976, *54* (4), 49–58.

Mintzberg, H., Raisighani, D., and Theoret, A. "The Structure of 'Unstructured' Decision Processes." *Administrative Science Quarterly,* 1976, *21* (2), 246–275.

Mitroff, I. I., and Kilmann, R. W. *Methodological Approaches to Social Science: Integrating Divergent Concepts and Theories.* San Francisco: Jossey-Bass, 1978.

Mitroff, I. I., and Mitroff, D. "Personality and Problem Solving: Making the Link Visible." *Journal of Experimental Learning and Simulation,* 1980, *2,* 111–119.

Morris, W. T. *Management for Action.* Reston, Va.: Reston Publishing, 1972.

Morrison, R. "The Chief Executive's Decision Making Dilemmas." *McKinsey Quarterly,* Summer 1973, pp. 19–33.

Murray, H. "The Personality and Career of Satan." *Journal of Social Issues,* 1962, *18* (4), 36–54.

Myers, I. B. *Manual for the Myers-Briggs Type Indicator.* Princeton, N.J.: Educational Testing Service, 1962.

Myers, I. B. *The Myers-Briggs Type Indicator: Manual and Supplements.* Palo Alto, Calif.: Consulting Psychologists Press, 1976.

Naisbitt, J. *Megatrends: Ten New Directions Transforming Our Lives.* New York: Warner Books, 1982.

Ohmae, K. *The Mind of the Strategist: The Art of Japanese Business.* New York: McGraw-Hill, 1982.

Okun, S. "An Ex-C.E.O., Jobless for 13 Months . . ." *New York Times,* Mar. 22, 1987, p. 12.

Ornstein, R. *The Psychology of Consciousness.* San Francisco: Freeman, 1975.

Ornstein, R. "The Split and Whole Brain." *Human Nature,* 1978, *1,* 76–83.

O'Toole, J. *Work in America.* Cambridge, Mass.: MIT Press, 1972.

O'Toole, J. *Vanguard Mangement: Redesigning the Corporate Future.* New York: Doubleday, 1985.

Peters, T. J., and Waterman, R. H., Jr. *In Search of Excellence: Lessons from America's Best-Run Companies.* New York: Harper & Row, 1982.

Posner, B. Z., and Schmidt, W. H. "Values and the American Manger: An Update." *California Management Review,* 1984, *26,* 202–216.

Powell, W., and Pedersen, D. "Can Corporate America Cope?" *Newsweek,* Nov. 17, 1986, pp. 64–65.

Restak, R. "The Hemispheres of the Brain Have Minds of Their Own." *New York Times,* Jan. 25, 1976, p. 8E.

Reynolds, R. S., Jr. "How to Pick a New Executive." *Fortune,* 1986, *114* (5), 113–114.

"The Right Executive for the Job: An Interview with Three Top Headhunters." *Business Forum,* Summer 1986, p. 23.

Roethlisberg, F. J., and Dickson, W. L. *Management and the Worker.* Cambridge, Mass.: Harvard University Press, 1939.

Rokeach, M. *The Open and Closed Mind.* New York: Basic Books, 1960.

Rowan, R. "The Best Managers Play Hunches." *U.S. News & World Report,* May 12, 1986a, p. 52.

Rowan, R. *The Intuitive Manager.* Boston: Little, Brown, 1986b.

Rowe, A. J. "The Myth of the Rational Decision Maker." *International Management,* Aug. 1974a, pp. 38–40.

Rowe, A. J. "Making Effective Decisions." *Chemical Engineering,* Sept. 16, 1974b, pp. 126–132.

Rowe, A. J. "Decision-Making in the 80's," *Los Angeles Business and Economics Journal,* Winter 1981, pp. 7–9.

Rowe, A. J., Bennis, W., and Boulgarides, J. D. "Desexing Decision Styles." *Personnel,* Jan.–Feb. 1984, pp. 43–52.

Rowe, A. J., and Boulgarides, J. D. "Decision Styles—A Perspective." *Learning and Organization Development Journal,* 1983, *4* (4), 3–9.

Rowe, A. J., and Cox, J. E. "The Decision Style Inventory—Theory, Use, and Validity." Dumfries, Va.: Starbird, 1986.

Rowe, A. J., and Mann, R. B. "Survival in the Eighties: How to Effectively Change Strategy." Unpublished manuscript, 1986.

Rowe, A. J., Mason, R. O., and Dickel, K. E. *Strategic Management and Business Policy: A Methodological Approach.* 2nd ed. Reading, Mass.: Addison-Wesley, 1985.

Rowe, A. J., Weingart, S. R., and Provenzano, R. J. *Navy Leadership Management Analysis Study.* Santa Monica, Calif.: Systems Development Corporation, 1977.

Russell, B., and Whitehead, A. N. *Principia Mathematica.* Cambridge, England: Cambridge University Press, 1913.

Sanoff, A. P. "Who Will Lead 'This New Breed' of Americans?" *U.S. News & World Report,* Mar. 15, 1982, pp. 80–81.

Sathe, V. *Culture and Related Corporate Realities.* Homewood, Ill.: Irwin, 1985.

Schroder, H. M., Driver, M. J., and Streufert, S. *Human Information Processing.* New York: Holt, Reinhart & Winston, 1967.

Sellers, P. "America's Most Admired Corporations." *Fortune,* Jan. 7, 1985, pp. 18–30.

Skinner, B. F. *Science and Human Behavior.* New York: Free Press, 1965.

Slocum, J. W., Jr., and Hellriegel, D. "A Look at How Managers' Minds Work." *Business Horizons,* July–Aug. 1983, pp. 58–68.

Smith, M. B. *Social Psychology and Human Value: Selected Essays.* Hawthorne, N.Y.: Aldine, 1969.

"The Sovereign State of ITT." *Business Week,* Aug. 11, 1973, pp. 15, 102.

Sperry, R. W. "Brain Bisection and Consciousness." In J. Eccles (ed.), *Brain and Conscious Experience.* New York: Springer-Verlag, 1966.

Sperry, R. W. "Hemisphere Deconnection and Unity in Conscious Awareness." *American Psychologist,* 1968, *23,* 723–733.

Springer, S. P., and Deutsch, G. *Left Brain, Right Brain.* San Francisco: Freeman, 1981.

Stevenson, H. H., and Gumpert, D. E. "The Heart of Entrepreneurship." *Harvard Business Review,* 1985, *63* (2), 85–94.

Streufert, S., Suedfeld, P., and Driver, M. "Conceptual Structure, Information Search and Information Utilization." *Journal of Personality and Social Psychology,* 1965, *2,* 736–740.

Stricker, L. J., and Ross, J. "Some Correlates of a Jungian Personality Inventory." *Psychological Reports,* 1964, *14,* 623–643.

Stryker, P. "Hidden Area of the President's Decision Making." *President's Association,* Special Study no. 25 Jan.–Feb. 1966, pp. 1–16.

Swinyard, A. W., and Bond, F. A. "Probing Opinions." *Harvard Business Review,* 1980, *58* (5), 6–11.

Szent-Gyorgyi, A. "Dionysians and Apollonians." *Science,* 1972, *176,* 966.

Tannenbaum, R., and Schmidt, H. "How to Choose a Leadership Pattern." *Harvard Business Review,* 1973, *51* (3), 167.

Taylor, R. W. *The Principles of Scientific Management.* New York: Harper & Row, 1947.

"They Call It 'Geneen U.'" *Forbes,* May 1, 1968, pp. 27–35.

Thompson, W. I. *At the Edge of History.* New York: Harper & Row, 1971.

Trowbridge, C. A., and Norris, F. D. "Selecting and Retaining Top Producers." *Real Estate Today,* Nov.–Dec. 1981, pp. 20–27.

Von Franz, M. *Lectures on Jung's Typology.* New York: Spring, 1971.

Wald, R. M., and Doty, R. A. "The Top Executive—A First Hand Profile." *Harvard Business Review,* 1954, *32* (4), 52.

Watson, T. J. *A Business and Its Beliefs: The Ideas That Helped Build IBM.* New York: McGraw-Hill, 1963.

Weick, K. E. "Managerial Thought in the Context of Action." In S. Srivastva and Associates, *The Executive Mind.* San Francisco: Jossey-Bass, 1984.

Weintraub, P. "The Brain: His and Hers." *Discover,* Apr. 1981, pp. 15–20.

"Wells Fargo Is Ready to Crack the Whip at Crocker." *Los Angeles Times,* Feb. 16, 1986, Sect. IV, pp. 1–2.

Wilhelm, R. *The I Ching, or Book of Changes.* 3rd ed. Translated by C. F. Baybes. Princeton, N.J.: Princeton University Press, 1967.

Williams, H. "Dedication: Why New Management is Needed." *New Management Magazine,* Spring 1983, p. 4.

Williamson, P. B. *Patton's Principles: A Handbook for Managers Who Mean It!* New York: Simon & Schuster, 1979.

Wilson, J. W. "The New Economy According to Drucker." *Business Week,* June 10, 1987, pp. 8–12.

Zakon, A. J. "Ten Rules for the CEO." In *Annual Perspective 1983.* Boston: Boston Consulting Group, 1983.

Zaleznick, A. "Power and Politics in Organizational Life." *Harvard Business Review,* 1970, *48* (3), 47–60.

Zaleznick, A. "Managers and Leaders: Are They Different?" *Harvard Business Review,* 1977, *55* (3), 67–78.

Index